THE CRUCIBLE OF FERMENT
New York's "Psychic Highway"

Emerson Klees

Cameo Press

Imprint of Friends of the Finger Lakes Publishing,

Rochester, New York, www.fingerlakes.com

Other books by Emerson Klees
Local interest books about the Finger Lakes Region
Persons, Places, and Things In the Finger Lakes Region (1993, 2000)
Persons, Places, and Things Around the Finger Lakes Region (1994)
People of the Finger Lakes Region (1995)
Legends and Stories of the Finger Lakes Region (1995)
The Erie Canal in the Finger Lakes Region (1996)
Underground Railroad Tales With Routes Through the Finger Lakes Region (1997)
More Legends and Stories of the Finger Lakes Region (1997)
The Women's Rights Movement and the Finger Lakes Region (1998)
Wineries of the Finger Lakes Region (2000)
Role Models of Human Values Series
One Plus One Equals Three—Pairing Man / Woman Strengths: Role Models of Teamwork (1998)
Entrepreneurs In History—Success vs. Failure: Entrepreneurial Role Models (1999)
Staying With It: Role Models of Perseverance (1999)

For information, write:

Friends of the Finger Lakes Publishing
P. O. Box 18131
Rochester, New York 14618

Library of Congress Control Number 2001126559

ISBN 1-891046-13-6

Printed in the United States of America
9 8 7 6 5 4 3 2 1

PREFACE

The Crucible of Ferment: New York's "Psychic Highway" highlights the religious fervor and social activism that occurred during the nineteenth century across a narrow band of New York State from southwest of Buffalo to Albany. This region was the crucible for an active ferment that had its origin in the social, religious, and economic activity across the State.

The activism that bubbled out of this crucible included the anti-Masonic movement, the temperance movement, the antislavery movement with accompanying underground railroad activity, and the women's rights movement. It is difficult to think of another area of the nation that encountered such restlessness. The haunting question is: "Why here? What was there about this region that caused such an intensity of emotion to occur here?"

One of the triggers of religious fervor in the region was the revival movement. The best-known revivalist of the first half of the nineteenth century was Charles Grandison Finney, a charismatic speaker who drew large crowds to his evangelist camp meetings.

Seven new religions, sects, and utopian communes were established along this narrow band across the State:

- Thomas Lake Harris and the Brotherhood of the New Life at Brocton
- William Miller and the Millerites, who predicted the end of the world
- Joseph Smith and the founding of Mormonism at Palmyra
- The Fox sisters and their experiences with Spiritualism at Hydesville
- Jemima Wilkinson, the Publick Universal Friend, and the Society of Universal Friends at Jerusalem, near Keuka Lake
- John Humphrey Noyes and the Oneida Community, near Utica
- Mother Ann Lee and the Shakers at Watervliet, near Albany.

These religions, sects, and communes are described in the body of the book. Their legacy is summarized in the epilogue. The prologue highlights the social, religious, and economic factors of the crucible of ferment and addresses the question: "Why here?" The introduction provides an overview of the activism that occurred in the area. Other communes and religions that originated in the region are described in the appendix. The glossary provides information about religions, sects, and communes referenced in the body of the book as well as definitions of religious terms.

LIST OF PHOTOGRAPHS

Cover design and illustration by Dunn and Rice Design, Inc., Rochester, New York

Map by Actionmaps, Rochester, New York

The [vector art] images used herein were obtained from IMSI's MasterClips Collection, 1895 Francisco Blvd. East, San Rafael, California 94901-5506, USA, and *The Clip Art Book* compiled by Gerard Quinn, New York: Cresent Books, 1990.

TABLE OF CONTENTS

COMPARISON OF SEVEN RELIGIONS, SECTS, AND COMMUNES

	Founder	Founded	Type of Organization
Harrisites (Brotherhood of the New Life)	Thomas Lake Harris (1823-1914)	1861, Wassaic, NY 1863, Amenia, NY 1867, Brocton, NY 1875, Santa Rosa, CA	Utopian commune; theocratic society; Christians who believed in Millennialism
Millerites	William Miller (1782-1849)	Low Hampton, NY	Adventist; members retained own relig-ion; based on the Bible—Revelation and Book of Daniel
Mormons (Church of Jesus Christ of Latter-day Saints)	Joseph Smith, Jr. (1805-1844)	1820, Palmyra, NY 1831, Kirtland, OH 1836, Jackson Co., MO 1839, Nauvoo, IL 1847, Salt Lake City	Christian religion, not Protestant; theo-cracy governed by twelve apostles; millennialists
Spiritualism	Kate Fox (1835-1892) Margaretta Fox (1834-1893)	1848, Hydesville, NY	Religious-philosoph-ical cult; creedless religion believing in "continuous life" and Davis's *Nature's Divine Revelations*
Society of Universal Friends	Jemima Wilkinson (1752-1819)	1776, New England 1787, Dresden, NY 1794, Jerusalem, NY	Religious sect; early converts were Quak-ers; community of individual landown-ers; millennialists
Oneida Community	John Humphrey Noyes (1811-1885)	1844, Putney, VT 1847, Oneida, NY	Communistic society of religious perfec-tionists, i.e. total cessation from sin; Bible Communists
Shakers (United Society of Believers in Christ's Second Appearing)	Mother Ann Lee (1736-1784) (in the U.S.) Jane and James Wardley	1774, New York, NY 1776, Watervliet, NY 1747, England	Sect that settled in communes; religious society; no paid min-isters; authority vest-ed in elders and dea-cons (men / women)

ALONG NEW YORK'S "PSYCHIC HIGHWAY"

Beliefs	Views on Marriage	Comments
That Harris would lead to a land of no sin, sorrow, or suffering—the center for world redemption; that the divine image was masculine / feminine	Marriages were spiritual, based on myths about sex; practiced celibacy until "free from lust"	Society in which human and celestial beings unite; early converts were Chrisians; most abandoned their religion.
That the end of the world would occur on April 23, 1843, then October 22, 1844, and that the raising of the righteous dead, the punishment of the wicked, and the extinction of evil followed	Millerites had no specific views about marriage.	Believed that at the last judgment God's kingdom will be established on earth; Adventism grew from Millerism.
That the Angel Moroni, the son of Mormon, gave Joseph Smith revelations; believe in atonement, the virgin birth, and immortality	Sanctioned polygamy from 1842 until 1890; celestial marriage is a relationship for eternity.	Tithing 10% of income is mandatory; missionary work for 2 years required; No alcohol, tobacco
That communication with those who live in the spirit world is possible; officials are mediums, ministers, and lay people; conducts investigations, analyses, and categorizations of phenomena	Spiritualism has no specific views about marriage.	Spiritualists are congregational, but not as ritualistic as Christian denominations; read from the Bible
Believed in the Separatist tradition of the Great Awakening; Jemima, who preached from the Bible, considered herself a "messenger of Christ."	Celibate, but didn't separate the sexes	Preached resignation, love, charity, and good works; believed in equality of the sexes
Believed that mutual criticism and freedom from materialism leads to Perfectionism; believed in freedom from sin—mankind already was redeemed (in AD 70)	Believed in union of spiritual man and woman for love w/o lust; complex marriage, all members married to all.	No formal religious ceremony; had lectures, readings and music; made human breeding tests
Believed in community of goods, nonresistance, divine government, confession, and power over disease; rejected atonement, the virgin birth, and the resurrection of the body; favored hymns over prayer	Celibate; sexes were separated, including married couples.	Women and men leaders; stressed chastity, honesty, temperance, labor, and cooperation

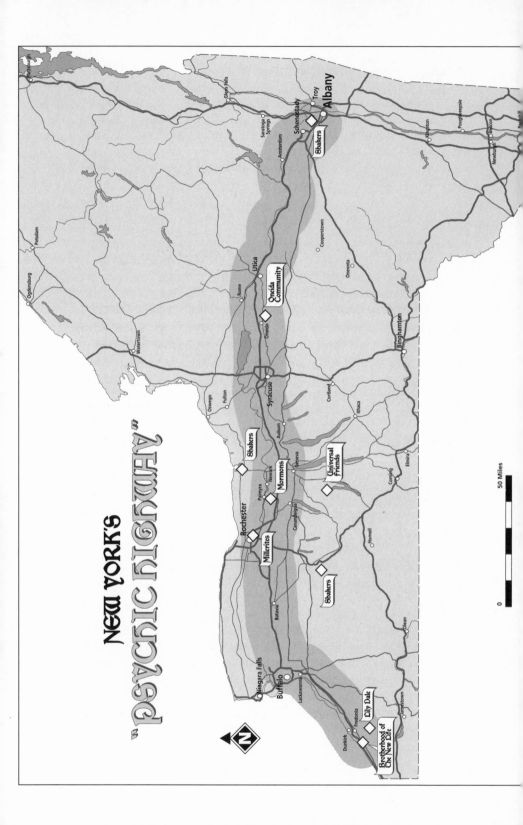

NEW YORK'S
"psychic highway"

Ogdensburg
Plattsburgh
Potsdam
Watertown
Glens Falls
Saratoga
Springs
Amsterdam
Troy
Albany
Schenectady
Shakers
Rome
Utica
Cooperstown
Oneida
Community
Oneida
Oneonta
Binghamton
Oswego
Fulton
Syracuse
Cortland
Ithaca
Auburn
Geneva
Universal
Friends
Elmira
Corning
Shakers
Newark
Palmyra
Mormons
Canandaigua
Rochester
Millerites
Hornell
Shakers
Batavia
Olean
Niagara Falls
Buffalo
Lackawanna
Fredonia
Dunkirk
Lily Dale
Jamestown
Brotherhood of
the New Life
Kingston
Poughkeepsie
Newburgh
Beacon
Peekskill

0   50 Miles

PROLOGUE

Social, Religious, and Economic Aspects
of the Crucible of Ferment

"Central and western New York became known as the 'Burned-over District' because a luxuriant growth of sects and cults sprang up after spiritual fires, presumably kindled by the Holy Spirit, swept over the region again and again. Why this region spawned such ardent religious excitement, so many eccentric opinions, and such unconventional behavior still puzzles historians. No doubt many citizens, having survived the backbreaking days of pioneering, had more time to nurture their hopes for a more perfect society in this world, certainly in the next. The speedup of transportation, the expansion of the religious as well as the secular press, and the rising levels of education also contributed to the rapid dissemination of religious and reform information.

The rising tension over states' rights, slavery, and immigration drove many to seek answers in Scripture or the writings of new prophets such as Joseph Smith. Upstaters, largely transplanted Yankees, awaited some sign from the Almighty, which several prophets were quick to supply. Emotionalism reached fever pitch and tens of thousands joined crusades against the Masons, the demon rum, and the slavocracy."[1]

David Maldwyn Ellis, *New York: State and City*

The "Psychic Highway"

In *Listen for a Lonesome Drum*, historian Carl Carmer referred to a "psychic highway" across New York State:

> Across the entire breadth of York State, unde-viatingly, a hilly strip scarcely twenty-five miles wide invites the world's wonder. It is a broad psychic highway, a thoroughfare of the occult whose great stations number the mystic seven. For where, in its rolling course from east of Albany to west of Buffalo, it has reached one of seven isolated and lonely heights, voices out of other worlds have spoken with spiritual authority to men and women, and the invisible mantles of the prophets have been laid on consecrated shoulders.
>
> In no other area of the Western Hemisphere have so many evidences of an existence transcending mortal living been manifest. It is impossible to reckon the number of listeners who on the plateaus of this strange midstate adventure have knelt before seen or unseen supernatural visitants to hear counsel. And the sum of those whose lives have been affected by that counsel, save for the fact that it is in the millions, is incalculable.[2]

At least ten new religions, sects, and communes were established along this narrow band across New York State. The "mystic seven" cited by Carl Carmer are:
- Thomas Lake Harris and the Brotherhood of the New Life on the shores of Lake Erie at Brocton, near Dunkirk
- William Miller and the Millerites who predicted the end of the world. Rochester was their western outpost.

- Joseph Smith and the founding of Mormonism at Palmyra
- The Fox sisters and their experiences with Spiritualism at Hydesville, near Newark
- Jemima Wilkinson, the Publick Universal Friend, and the Society of Universal Friends at Jerusalem, near Keuka Lake
- John Humphrey Noyes and the Oneida Community, near Utica
- Mother Ann Lee and the Shakers at Watervliet, near Albany, with communities at Sodus and Groveland in the Finger Lakes Region

The Burned-over District

"The Burned-over District" is the name applied to New York State along Lake Ontario to the Adirondacks during the first half of the nineteenth century. The name refers to a region that experienced a large number of religious revivals.

Whitney R. Cross described it in *The Burned-over District: The Social and Intellectual History of Enthusiastic Religion in Western New York, 1800-1850*:

> Across the rolling hills of western New York and along the line of DeWitt Clinton's famed Erie Canal, there stretched in the second quarter of the nineteenth century, a "psychic highway." Upon this broad belt of land congregated a people extraordinarily given to unusual religious beliefs, particularly devoted to crusades aimed at the perfection of mankind and the attainment of millennial happiness. Few of the enthusiasms or eccentricities of this generation of Americans failed to find exponents here. Most of them gained rather more support here than elsewhere. Several originated in the region....

Critics chiefly concerned with the habitual revivalism occurring in a much wider area came to call it the "Burnt" or "Burned-over District," adopting the prevailing western analogy between the fires of the forest and those of the spirit. Charles Grandison Finney, the greatest evangelist of the day, helped give it its customary usage when he applied it to localities between Lake Ontario and the Adirondacks where early Methodist circuit riders had, he thought, left souls hardened against proper religious tutelage....[3]

In addition, central and western New York State were the hub of the anti-Masonic movement between 1826 and the mid-1830s. The region was a hotbed of the temperance movement and the abolitionist movement including the underground railroad, and it was the birthplace of the women's rights movement in the United States.

Why were central and western New York so susceptible to this religious fervor and social activism? In order to understand why this agrarian region encountered such restlessness, one must look at the settlers of the region, where they came from, the religious background they brought with them, and the social and economic conditions that they encountered.

Social Factors

Social factors that contributed to the unrest in the region were a high degree of social (vertical) mobility, considerable geographical (horizontal) mobility, a constant flow of immigrants into the region with a mix of cultural backgrounds, the impact of the growth of commercial agriculture, and, eventually, industrialization that disrupted culture patterns. Leaders that emerged in the region to drive the various social experiments and reform movements were major contributors to the crucible of ferment.

Settlement in central New York State began in the late 1780s and was dominated by Yankees from New England. Many pioneers came up the Susquehanna River from Pennsylvania to settle in southern tier counties. Most of the New Englanders settled first in eastern New York counties and then pulled up stakes and resettled in the central and western regions of the State. Few pioneers came from Boston or the fertile Connecticut River Valley; many came from the hill country of New Hampshire and Vermont and from other areas of Massachusetts and Connecticut.

Many pioneers who moved to New York from New England were the ambitious younger sons of the family with limited prospects on the family's hardscrabble farm. Because of their youth, they were caught up in a spirit of adventure, were more willing to take risks, and were not afraid of challenges. Eventually, a gradual shift to commercial agriculture freed many pioneer children from farm chores, permitting them to spend more time on education and religious activities.

College attendance increased significantly throughout the first half of the nineteenth century. In 1829, more New Yorkers went to college than residents of Pennsylvania and New Jersey combined. Over half the New Yorkers attended college in their home state; most of the remainder went to New England colleges. After 1835, many western New Yorkers attended Oberlin College in Ohio, where Charles Grandison Finney was a member of the faculty.

In *Religion in America*, Winthrop S. Hudson comments on factors contributing to the crucible of ferment:

> The first half of the nineteenth century in the United States was a time of eager expectancy, unbridled enthusiasm, and restless ferment. A new nation and a new world were being born, and to many anything and everything were possible. It was a period when a comet's tail was said to have swept America, and everyone

13

went a little mad....

Two factors combined to produce the unusual religious ferment of these years. One was the social context. The other was the religious climate. In the American environment, there was an absence of tradition and a sense of pregnant possibility which encouraged the spirit of experimentation. Nor was this experimentation inhibited by law. Unlimited freedom had been granted religious expression, no matter how eccentric it might be.

And an abundance of cheap land and open space provided an unequaled opportunity to implement and institutionalize religious ideas. If the context was hospitable to innovation, the actual impetus that gave rise to most of the novel cults, sects, and movements was the climate of opinion generated by successive waves of revivalism.[4]

Religious Factors

Many of the settlers from New England were Baptists, Congregationalists, or Methodists. Presbyterians and one branch of Congregationialists merged in 1801 in the Plan of Union. All major denominations, except Episcopalians, were revivalistic. Baptists and Methodists were more emotional and easier for common people to understand than Presbyterians.

An increase in religious revivals in 1826 in central and western New York is credited to the influence of Charles Grandison Finney, a highly motivational speaker. This increase in activity continued from 1826 through 1837.

REVIVALS

Revivalism was viewed as a return to religion, e.g. to be born again, and as an awakening of new church members. Religious fervor and mass evangelism were elements of revivalism. From 1815 to 1818, six revivals were held in Rhode Island, fifteen in Connecticut, twenty-one each in New Jersey, eastern New York, and Pennsylvania, forty-five in Vermont, sixty-four in Massachusetts, and eighty in the Burned-over District.

Charles Grandison Finney was the most prominent evangelist of the Second Great Awakening in the United States (1800 to 1835). He spoke out against urbanization and industrial revolution and advocated a return to a more simple, pious life.

In 1831, Finney came to Rochester for a revivalist meeting that was one of the largest until that time. His sermons included "The Carnal Mind Is Enmity Against God" and "The Wages of Sin Is Death." Finney's impact on the region's emotional intensity was significant:

> Charles G. Finney and his colleagues not only converted hundreds of thousands but stimulated many reform movements. Upstate became the nursery for many humanitarian movements. Among the reformers were Theodore Weld and Gerrit Smith, who sought to abolish slavery; Elizabeth Cady Stanton and Susan B. Anthony, persistent fighters for women's rights; and John B. Gough, a reformed drunkard who enthralled thousands with his lurid tales of degradation. Finney attracted support from such wealthy men as the Tappan brothers, silk merchants in New York City....[5]

The next peak in revivalism came in 1837, a year of recession. Interest in the church always increased in bad times.

The religious fervor of the region burned itself out over the last half of the nineteenth century. Nevertheless, some of the legacies of the Burned-over District survived into the twenty-first century: the Mormon Church; several Adventist denominations, including the Seventh-day Adventists; two species of Methodism, including the Free Methodists; and some Spiritualist groups. The American tradition was enriched by these legacies, which led to modern versions of religion.

Economic Factors

THE ERIE CANAL

On July 4, 1817, construction of the Erie Canal along a 364-mile route from Albany to Buffalo began at Rome. The ninety-four-mile section of the canal from Rome west to the Seneca River was chosen to be constructed first because it had a long, flat stretch of favorable terrain that required only six locks. The ditch of the original canal was forty feet wide at the top, twenty-eight feet wide at the bottom, and only four feet deep.

In October 1819, a crowd gathered at Rome to celebrate the opening of the first section of the canal, the fifteen miles between Rome and Utica. On July 4, 1820, seventy-three new canalboats left Syracuse for Rome to celebrate the completion of the middle section of the canal.

The canal from Rochester to Albany was opened in 1823; the cost of shipping a barrel of flour between those two cities dropped from $3.00 to $.75. The full length of the Erie Canal was opened in 1825 with the ceremonial Buffalo to Albany cruise of Governor DeWitt Clinton on the *Seneca Chief*, accompanied by four other canalboats. Completion of the Erie Canal brought significant economic and social changes.

•   •   •

Population growth was phenomenal in the 1820s: Albany grew by 96 percent, Buffalo by 314 percent, Rochester by 512 percent, Syracuse by 282 percent, and Utica by 183 percent.

The Genesee Valley region became the nation's main grain-growing region. Rochester was considered the first inland boom town. Land speculation and boom-town construction projects were rampant.

During the second half of the nineteenth century, social, religious, and economic conditions began to change. The factors that led to the Civil War were the root of many of these changes, including different social environments, one slave and one free, upon which two economic systems were based. The Civil War had many profound impacts on the nation, one of which was the increase in industrialization.

The antislavery crusade became the principal reform movement, thrusting aside, at least temporarily, the temperance and women's rights movements. Following the Civil War, the country was swept by expansion in the money markets of capitalism, increase in population with the large influx of immigrants, and the accompanying urbanization. Later in the century, when new waves of humanitarianism occurred, the reform movements were different because the social and economic conditions had changed.

The religious fervor and the reform movements in central and western New York played important roles in the growth of the new republic during the first full century of its existence. In *Freedom's Ferment*, Alice Felt Tyler comments on the impact of these activities:

> For too long, we have paid amused attention to the fads and fancies of the early nineteenth century. Phrenology, hydropathy, mesmerism, health and diet notions, free love, spiritual affinities, and all the other eccentricities of the era have had more than their due share of limelight. Alongside them were fundamentals of faith, crusades, reforms, and reformers whose effect on American civilization is profound and permanent.

The bases of our social history were well laid and deep; there is more than froth in our heritage of the past. The religious movements and the adventures in reform of the early years of the republic were the truly significant activities of the men and women of the age, and they contributed much to the way of life of twentieth-century America [and beyond].[6]

Determining conclusively why this religious activity and social experimentation occurred in central and western New York in the nineteenth century is difficult; nevertheless, describing the social, religious, and economic factors that created the environment in which it happened help to explain it. The door has been left open for future historians to expand upon the explanation.

INTRODUCTION

Activism in the Crucible of Ferment

"A period of intense sectarian activity occurred between 1800 and 1850 in upper New York State.... The first half of the nineteenth century saw such a flurry of sectarian activity in New York, so many 'luxuriant new growths,' that the area earned for itself the name of 'Burned-over District....' This surge of sectarianism started, as so many do, with a wave of revivalism which began about 1800. All the major denominations (with the exception of Episcopalianism) were affected. The Second Great Awakening, with its camp meetings, itinerant preachers, and interdenominational missions, reached its peak in this area between 1825 and 1837. Not only did new members flock to the established denominations, but many splinter Baptist and Methodist groups were formed.

In addition, ... it was also a period of widespread religious experimentation. Not only did marginal groups like the Shakers attract renewed attention, but new sects were formed at this time, including the Mormons, the Millerites, and various Spiritualist circles. Added to this was the ferment caused by the widely popular temperance, abolitionist, and anti-Masonry movements that swept the area during those years."[7]

John Wilson, *Religion in American Society: The Effective Presence*

Activism in central and western New York during the nineteenth century included the anti-Masonic movement, the temperance movement, the antislavery movement with the underground railroad, and the women's rights movement. Of these four reform movements, the anti-Masonic movement was a somewhat localized activity over a relatively short period of time; the other three were active over a long period of time and over a wide area of the country:

- Anti-Masonic movement—from 1827, shortly after the abduction of Mason antagonist William Morgan in Canandaigua, to the mid-1830s when interest in the Anti-Masonic Party waned in U.S. politics, and the party was absorbed by the Whig Party. The most active area of the anti-Masonic movement was from the Finger Lakes Region to the Niagara Frontier; the movement also flourished in New England, in the other Middle Atlantic States, and in northeastern Ohio.
- Temperance movement—from colonial times until the beginning of Prohibition in 1920.
- Antislavery movement—from early Quaker activity in the late eighteenth century until the signing of the Emancipation Proclamation in 1863 and the end of the Civil War in 1865. Quakers began to aid escaped slaves early in the nineteenth century. In 1830, the activity increased, and the effort, which was given the name "underground railroad," continued until the end of the first year of the Civil War when escaped slaves were taken in behind Union lines.
- Women's rights movement—from the first women's rights conference in Seneca Falls in July 1848 until 1920, when the "Susan B. Anthony Amendment" to the Constitution was ratified.

Anti-Masonic Movement
The anti-Masonic movement was a reaction to the treatment of one of its members, William Morgan, who was abducted

by the Masons and apparently murdered for publishing the rituals of their first three orders in his book, *Illustrations of Masonry.*

In *Freedom's Ferment*, Alice Felt Tyler discusses the nature of the movement:

> It was only through the assertion that Freemasonry was secret, undemocratic, and subversive of American institutions that support could be acquired for the proscription of the Masonic order, and discrimination against the foreign born was justified by charges that immigrants neither understood the responsibilities of American citizenship nor appreciated its privileges....

> Social and economic in its origin but largely political in its expression, the attack on the Masonic order in the years after 1827 was an extraordinary manifestation of the combination of principle, prejudice, and hysteria that has often confounded students of American democracy. Perhaps it was no coincidence that this movement began in the "burnt" district of [central and] western New York, which had been fed by the flames of the Great Revival.[8]

The William Morgan incident occurred at a time of rapid economic expansion in western New York, principally due to the completion of the Erie Canal in 1825, and at a time when the rural populace was beginning to rebel against the middle class that controlled politics in the villages and towns. *In The Burned-over District*, Whitney R. Cross explains the reasons for anti-Masonic feelings:

> In its original form, and persistently in rural

areas, anti-Masonry was a crusade, with marked affinity for most of the movements in the region and reform which would make western New York distinctive in coming years. The major issue seemed to be one of morality; Masonry was believed to have committed a crime. Its members had put their fraternal obligations ahead of their duty to state and society, sanctioning both a lawless violation of personal security and a corrupt plot to frustrate the normal constitutional guarantees of justice.[9]

Churches began to take action against the Masons. Ministers who belonged to the fraternal organization were asked to resign their membership. In Vermont, members of the Baptist, Methodist, and Disciples of Christ Churches were the most avid anti-Masons.

A new political party, the Anti-Masonic Party, was formed, and 112 delegates, including eleven ex-Masons from eleven states, attended its initial meeting. In 1830, William H. Seward ran for the New York State Senate as the candidate of the Anti-Masonic Party.

In 1831, the Anti-Masonic Party met in Baltimore to pick a candidate for President of the United States. They were the first third party in the United States, the first party to hold a nominating convention, and the first to publish a platform of party principles.

During the years of anti-Masonic fervor, the number of Masonic lodges in New York State declined from 360 in 1826 to seventy-five in 1836; membership dropped from 22,000 to 4,000 over that ten-year period. Revivalist Charles Grandison Finney estimated that 2,000 Masonic lodges ceased their fraternal activity, and 45,000 Masons suspended their membership in the fraternal order during that time.

Although central and western New York were the most

active regions for the anti-Masonic movement, the Anti-Masonic Party was active in other states as well. Thaddeus Stevens was a member of the party in Pennsylvania, and, in 1833, ex-President John Quincy Adams ran for governor of Massachusetts as a candidate of the Anti-Masonic Party.

Temperance Movement

Battles against demon rum had occurred in the United States since colonial times. Drinking was viewed as a cause of unhappy marriages, health problems, and criminal behavior. The temperance movement picked up momentum during the 1820s when evangelists began to preach the need for reform.

Motivated by sermons of Charles Grandison Finney and Lyman Beecher of Litchfield, Connecticut, reformers established temperance societies. Beecher's *Six Sermons on Intemperance* addressed "the banishment of ardent spirits from the list of lawful articles of commerce by a correct and efficient public sentiment." Dr. Benjamin Rush was an early advocate of temperance. His *Inquiry into the Effect of Ardent Spirits upon the Human Mind and Body* was a bestseller. *Drunkard's Looking Glass* by Peter Weems also offered advice against drinking.

The Presbyterian Church, the Dutch Reformed Church, and the Methodist Church were among the early denominations preaching against the distillation and sale of alcoholic beverages. In 1829, the New York Temperance Society was founded. The Society provided lecturers to speak out against drunkenness and distributed hundreds of thousands of pamphlets about the ills of drinking. One of its early efforts was to tighten the system of granting licenses to taverns. By 1850, the society claimed over 100,000 members.

The "experience speech," in which a reformed drinker discussed his struggle with alcohol, became a feature of temperance oratory. John Gough, who impressed Susan B. Anthony with his speaking style, was a reformed drunkard who became a professional temperance orator.

An early issue of the temperance movement was whether or not total abstinence from all alcoholic beverages should be advocated. Many believers in temperance were against the drinking of liquor but felt that wine, beer, and hard cider used in moderation were not intoxicating. The word "teetotaler" originated in Hector on Seneca Lake.

In 1818, the local temperance society was split into two camps, one that wanted the abstinence pledge to be a total one, including beer, wine, and hard cider, and another that just wanted to stop the consumption of distilled alcoholic beverages, such as whiskey. When the vote was recorded, the recorder marked a "T" next to names of those who were for total abstinence. They became known as "T-Totalers."

In 1851, the Maine Legislature passed a statewide prohibition law that contained the strongest wording of any temperance effort until that time. The law banned the manufacture and sale of alcoholic beverages by wholesalers and retailers. Liquor required for medicinal purposes was available only through bonded agents. The Maine Law provided for the seizure of illegal alcoholic beverages and made it easier to prosecute violators. Between 1852 and 1855, twelve additional states, including New York, passed legislation similar to the Maine Law. The temperance movement continued into the twentieth century, resulting in Prohibition in 1920.

Antislavery Movement

In April 1775, the first abolitionist society was established in Pennsylvania. The society's first president was Benjamin Franklin. States began to pass laws abolishing slavery in the late eighteenth century.

In 1831, the New England Anti-Slavery Society was organized by twelve Bostonians, including William Lloyd Garrison, editor of the antislavery newspaper, *The Liberator.* In 1833, the American Anti-Slavery Society was formed in Philadelphia. Including abolitionist William Still, three of the sixty-two founders were African Americans.

In October 1835, New York antislavery activists convened in Utica to form a state antislavery society. Conservatives broke up the meeting of 600 delegates held in the Second Presbyterian Church. Organized as the New York Anti-Slavery Society, the delegates reconvened at Temperance House and appointed Gerrit Smith as chairman of a committee to schedule the next meeting. He scheduled the meeting for the following day at Peterboro, his home town, and 300-400 delegates attended.

Smith observed that free and open discussion was being threatened, not for a good purpose, but to support oppression; to ensure that "two millions and a half of our fellow men, crushed in the iron folds of slavery, may remain in all their suffering and debasement and despair."

Furthermore, he commented that the suppression of free discussion at Utica verified what thinking people everywhere knew, "that slavery cannot live, unless the North be tongue-tied." In July 1836, he was commissioned as an agent of the American Anti-Slavery Society to conduct meetings and establish auxiliary societies.

In 1839, Theodore Weld published *American Slavery As It Is: Testimony of a Thousand Witnesses*, which provided source material for lecturers on antislavery. Weld was married to Angelina Grimké, who with her sister, Sarah, were among the first women to speak in public.

Another antislavery activist was Frederick Douglass, who had been born into slavery in Maryland. In 1838, Douglass escaped to New Bedford, Massachusetts, by way of Philadelphia and New York. One day he found a copy of William Lloyd Garrison's antislavery newspaper, *The Liberator*, and it changed his life. Garrison was a strong-willed abolitionist. Douglass accepted an assignment with the New England Anti-Slavery Society, improved his oratorical skills, and became one of the Society's most popular lecturers.

Douglass moved to Rochester, a booming city of 30,000

on the Erie Canal, where he had been well-received on the lecture circuit, to publish an antislavery newspaper. The leading abolitionist of central New York, Gerrit Smith, supported him and gave him the deed to forty acres of land near Rochester. Douglass moved his family there on November 1, 1847. On December 3, the first edition of his newspaper, *North Star*, was published. He named the paper *North Star* because the north star was the guide that the slaves used when escaping from the South to freedom.

Central and western New York were significant participants in the antislavery movement. Just how significant is summarized by Whitney R. Cross in *The Burned-over District*:

> The burned-over district seized leadership in the abolition crusade, and the consequent influence of the region upon the enlarged anti-slavery agitation of the forties and fifties and upon the Civil War itself, constitutes the most important single contribution of western New York's enthusiastic mood to the main currents of American history.[10]

Underground Railroad

Among the most active in helping fugitive slaves was the Society of Friends, or Quakers. In Germantown, Pennsylvania, Quakers made one of the earliest position statements on the subject: "There is a saying, that we shall do to all men like as we will be done to ourselves; making no difference of what the generation, descent or color they are."

The Quakers believed that no man or woman should be owned by another. By 1782, all Quaker-owned slaves had been given their freedom. Because they disagreed with the fugitive slave laws, they began to disobey them peacefully; they provided whatever help to slaves that they could. In 1804, Quakers in Columbia, Pennsylvania, rescued an escaped slave who had been a victim of a slave agent's cruelty. The operation organized by the Quakers to help fugitive slaves eventually became known as the underground railroad.

Baptist congregations established societies to aid the slaves; Presbyterian churches supported their education; and the Congregationalist church was very active in helping the fugitives. In 1835, Congregationalists established a college and a colony for escaped slaves in Oberlin, Ohio.

The scale of operations of the underground railroad expanded considerably beginning around 1830. The origin of the name can be traced to 1831 when a fugitive, Tice Davids, escaped his pursuers, including his master, after crossing the Ohio River near Ripley, Ohio. By the time his master had found a skiff and crossed the River, Davids was out of sight. When his master inquired in nearby Ripley, he was told, "He must have gone off on an underground road." The story was repeated frequently and, ultimately, gave the name to the line. In 1831, railroad trains powered by steam engines began operating in the United States. It is likely that the term "underground road" became "underground railroad" after that time.

The underground railroad developed a set of titles for its participants. An "agent" was anyone who worked on the underground railroad. The fugitive slaves were temporarily housed in "stations," and the owner of the station was a "stationmaster." Those who accompanied the escaped slaves to the next station were "conductors." The larger underground railroad organizations had "managers" or "presidents." Individuals who contributed money for clothing, food, and transportation were called "stockholders."

Stations were usually between ten and twenty miles apart. The average distance between stations was twelve miles, which was the distance that healthy slaves could walk or that a wagon could travel overnight. All travel was done at night, except in emergencies.

Elmira, Albany, Syracuse, Rochester, Buffalo, and Ithaca were active hubs on the underground railroad. One of the principal underground railroad routes to New York State was from Philadelphia to Elmira, where John Jones, an escaped slave, was the stationmaster. Mark Twain's father-in-law, Jervis Langdon, was a "stockholder" of the underground railroad in Elmira. From Elmira, the underground railroad ran northeasterly to Albany and New England, north to Ithaca or Syracuse, and northwesterly to Rochester.

From Ithaca, at least five northerly routes were used to transport slaves. One of the routes was by boat on Cayuga Lake. From Syracuse, escaped slaves went west to Rochester or north to Oswego and across Lake Ontario to Canada. From Rochester, fugitives either were transported west to Buffalo or across Lake Ontario to Canada. From Buffalo, escaped slaves were taken across the Niagara River to Canada. St. Catharines, Ontario, was a popular destination.

In 1850, the Fugitive Slave Law was passed, allowing slavecatchers and slaveowners to return escaped slaves to the South without much of a hearing. After 1850, many more slaves went to Canada where they could not be returned to their plantations. Estimates of the total number of slaves that escaped to the North, not just those who went through New York State, range from 40,000 to 100,000.

Women's Rights Movement

Women played an active role in the temperance and abolition movements early in the nineteenth century. Meetings were held, pamphlets were written, and societies were formed to address the evils of drinking and slavery. Women became actively involved in both movements but were not welcomed into the temperance or antislavery societies, so they formed their own. Susan B. Anthony founded the Women's State Temperance Association after being denied the opportunity to speak at a Sons of Temperance meeting, and Lucretia Mott was one of the founders of the Philadelphia Female Anti-Slavery Society.

These female societies provided good training for those

who later were active in the women's rights movement. Virtually all of the early women's rights leaders learned how to organize and to work together in the temperance and anti-slavery movements. They learned how to prepare and circulate petitions, to plan and hold conventions, and to handle the considerable volume of criticism that they received.

They gained valuable experience in speaking before audiences. The early speeches were given to other women in parlors on the topics of temperance and antislavery. The first women's rights convention in Seneca Falls on July 19-20, 1848, is considered the beginning of the women's rights movement in the United States.

In 1854, Elizabeth Cady Stanton made her first address to the New York State Legislature on the Married Woman's Property Act and women's suffrage. Six years later she again addressed the State Legislature to request the expansion of married women's rights and women's suffrage.

In 1863, the National Woman's Loyal League was established by Susan B. Anthony and Elizabeth Cady Stanton. In 1868, the division between two factions of the women's rights movement widened; one wanted to wait for African-American men to get the vote before votes for women were pursued, and one didn't. In the following year, the break occurred between the two factions.

Women who agreed with Susan B. Anthony and Elizabeth Cady Stanton met to organize the National Woman Suffrage Association to work for the passage of an amendment to the Constitution granting the vote to women. In November 1869, Lucy Stone and her New Englanders formed the American Woman Suffrage Association.

In 1872, Susan B. Anthony was arrested for attempting to vote in a national election in Rochester. Her trial in the Ontario County Courthouse in Canandaigua drew national attention because of the unjust treatment that she received. After sentencing, she refused to pay her fine, saying, "I shall never pay a dollar of your unjust penalty."

In 1890, the American and the National Woman Suffrage Associations reunited as the National American Woman Suffrage Association. Elizabeth Cady Stanton was elected president; Susan B. Anthony became vice president; and Lucy Stone was head of the executive committee.

Seventy-two years passed before the Amendment to the Constitution granting women's rights was ratified in 1920. The leaders of the movement in its early years, Lucretia Mott, Elizabeth Stanton, Lucy Stone, and Susan B. Anthony were not around in the second decade of the twentieth century. They had turned the leadership of the movement over to Carrie Chapman Catt, Alice Paul, and others.

STORIES ABOUT ACTIVISM

Anti-Masonic Movement

William Morgan's story is the story of the anti-Masonic movement. He was admitted to the Wells lodge of the Masons in Rochester as a visitor and awarded membership in the Royal Arch Masons in Le Roy.

Morgan broke with the Masonic Order when he wasn't hired to work on the Masonic lodge being built in Le Roy. In 1826, he moved to Batavia and applied for membership in a Royal Arch Masons chapter being formed. Officials knew Morgan as one who had more than an occasional drink, and who was a loose talker. They denied him membership. Thereafter, he was determined to get even with the Masons.

Morgan decided to publish the secrets of the order with the help of David C. Miller, publisher of the Batavia *Republican-Advocate*. Miller had received the first degree of the Masonic Order; Morgan had received the first three degrees. The Masons became aroused by Morgan's threat to reveal the first three degrees of the order, and they tried to talk him out of it.

Susan B. Anthony

Miller and Morgan were prosecuted for debts, but they raised bail and stayed out of jail. Attempts were made to burn down the building that housed Miller's press. Morgan was served a warrant on September 11, 1826, for petty theft from a Canandaigua tavernkeeper. He was taken to Canandaigua where the charge was dismissed. He was then jailed in Canandaigua for a small debt owed to another Canandaigua innkeeper. Four Masons paid the debt and secured Morgan's release.

The four men seized Morgan as he left the jail and led him to a carriage. Morgan lost his hat in a minor scuffle and was heard crying out, "Murder." Morgan was taken to Fort Niagara, where he was kept in the powder magazine until arrangements could be made to send him to Canada. His "guard" rowed him across the Niagara River, but the Canadians didn't want him either. Morgan was never heard from again.

People asked, "Where is William Morgan?" An anti-Masonic movement began to build. The full title of Morgan's book is *Illustrations of Masonry by One of the Fraternity Who Has Devoted Thirty Years to the Subject*. Sales were sluggish; people were more interested in what happened to Morgan than they were in his exposé of passwords and secret grips.

Morgan's body was never found. With no *corpus delicti*, no proof of death, no one could be charged with his murder. Nevertheless, Thurlow Weed, a Rochester editor, pried information from John Whitney, one of Morgan's abductors. Whitney told Weed that Morgan had been promised a farm in Canada, so he willingly went out in a rowboat on the Niagara River.

When they were out on the river, his captors tied a rope around him with a weight on the other end. Morgan struggled and bit off the thumb of one of his captors, but they maneuvered him into the river. Whitney never signed a confession of the incident; nothing could be proved in court.

Morgan's four abductors were convicted of kidnapping

Morgan from the Canandaigua jail. All served brief jail terms. Twelve indictments were handed down at trials in Genesee, Monroe, Niagara, and Ontario counties, and Sheriff Bruce of Niagara County spent over two years in jail. Whitney was jailed for one year and three months, and others served short jail terms. Sixty-nine Masons were involved in the abduction. Their action had an unanticipated, adverse impact on their fraternal order. Membership in Masonic lodges declined dramatically in the region.

Temperance Movement

In January 1852, all temperance societies of New York assembled at a convention in Albany. When Susan B. Anthony asked to speak, she was told that ladies had been invited to listen, not to participate. Anthony and others withdrew to form their own organization, the Women's State Temperance Association.

Elizabeth Cady Stanton was elected president; Antoinette Brown, the first woman minister, and Mrs. Gerrit Smith were elected vice presidents. Susan B. Anthony and Amelia Bloomer were elected secretaries. The leaders of the women's rights movement had become the leaders of the Women's State Temperance Association.

In 1853, Abby Kelly Foster attempted to speak at the World's Temperance Convention in New York City but was drowned out by male attendees. Antislavery and temperance activist Wendell Phillips accompanied Antoinette Brown to the convention hall to present her credentials. The presiding chairman invited her to speak. However, delegates to the convention shouted her down for an hour an a half. After this treatment, many leaders of the reform movement, men and women, diverted their efforts to causes other than temperance.

The women of New York State fought demon rum with the spoken word. It didn't occur to them to take a more physical approach to reform, as Carrie Nation did at a much later time. On January 21, 1901, Carrie Nation and three of her "assistants" stormed into James Burns's saloon in Wichita, Kansas, and demolished the bar and the interior with hatchets before moving on to a second saloon where the owner waved a revolver to persuade them to stop their destruction. Upstate New York women pursued a much more rational course of action.

Antislavery Movement

The story of the Jerry Rescue is an example of the region's involvement in the antislavery movement. On October 1, 1851, the streets of Syracuse were crowded with visitors. Many abolitionists were visiting the city to attend the convention of the National Liberty Party, and other visitors had come for the Onondaga County Fair. Just as the convention delegates were finishing lunch, the bell of the Congregationalist Church began to peal. The Vigilance Committee recognized the signal that a fugitive was in danger. Other church bells began to ring, and soon city buildings were emptied of their inhabitants.

Everyone headed for the office of Joseph F. Sabine, Commissioner of the United States Circuit Court, in the Townsend block. William Henry, also known as Jerry McHenry, had been arrested by Deputy U.S. Marshal Allen and accused of being a runaway slave.

Jerry was a forty-year-old African American who worked at a cooper's shop in Syracuse. His mother was Celia, a slave from North Carolina. Jerry, a red-headed mulatto, was thought to be the son of his master.

Commissioner Sabine's office was surrounded by a large crowd. Before the charges could be read to Jerry, he ran away from his captors. He was shackled, but he outdistanced his pursuers for about a half mile down the street. When they caught him, he fought back and suffered a cracked rib and severe bruises. Edward Sheldon, founder of the Oswego Normal School, observed of Jerry's recapture, "I saw this fugitive from, not justice, but injustice, dragged through the streets like a dog, every rag of clothes stripped from his back, hauled upon a cart like a dead carcass, and driven away to a police office for a mock trial."

At the police station, Reverend Samuel May of the Unitarian Church calmed the agitated captive by telling him that an escape was being planned. Reverend May then joined a meeting of the Vigilance Committee. Meanwhile Marshal Allen, who was expecting trouble, called upon the Onondaga County Sheriff, William Gardner, for assistance.

Commissioner Sabine opened Jerry's hearing at 5:30 p.m. The large crowd gathered outside of the building continually interrupted the proceedings with yelling and rock-throwing. A National Liberty Party delegate from Michigan spoke to the crowd in an attempt to calm them. Jerry's defense attorney tried to convince that crowd to go home because Jerry would be freed by legal process.

Samuel Ward, an African-American Congregationalist minister, also addressed the crowd, "We are witnessing such a sight as, I pray, we may never look upon again. A man in chains, in Syracuse! ... They say he is a slave. What a term to apply to an American! How does this sound beneath the pole of liberty and the flag of freedom?"

At dusk, the Vigilance Committee emerged from their meeting, collected their clubs and a battering ram, and headed for the police station where Jerry was shouting that he would rather die than be returned to slavery. The gas lights were turned off, and the doors and windows in the police station were smashed. Marshal Fitch from Rochester, who had joined Marshal Swift of Auburn and Marshal Bemis of Canandaigua in support of Marshal Allen, fired two shots, jumped thirteen feet out of a second story window, and broke his arm.

Jerry, who was too injured to walk, was carried to a waiting carriage and driven to the home of an African-American family, where his shackles were removed. From there, he was moved to the home of a pro-slavery advocate whose house was not likely to be searched. Jerry stayed there for four days until his wounds healed, and then he was transported to a farm in Mexico, Oswego County.

All vessels leaving New York for Canada were searched by U.S. Marshals; it was difficult to make arrangements for Jerry's passage across Lake Ontario. Finally, the captain of an English cargo ship with a load of lumber agreed to provide passage for him. The owner of a sawmill and tannery in Mexico shipped Jerry as a "consignment of boots and shoes" to Oswego, where he was smuggled aboard the cargo vessel. Jerry arrived safely in Kingston, Ontario, and found a job in a furniture factory. He wrote to those who had helped him escape and thanked them for their help.

Not everyone agreed with the actions of the Vigilance Committee. Many citizens were concerned with the Committee's taking the law into its own hands. The newspapers of Albany, Buffalo, Rochester, Syracuse, and Utica universally condemned the actions of the Committee. Reverend Samuel May, formerly a pacifist, favored open conflict when required to bring change. He wrote to New England abolitionist William Lloyd Garrison, "I have seen that it was necessary to bring people into direct conflict with the Government—that the Government may be made to understand that it has transcended its limits—and must recede."

Underground Railroad
HARRIET TUBMAN

Harriet Tubman was called "the Moses of her people." In 1860, she made her last journey on the underground railroad. In nineteen trips, she led over 300 slaves to freedom. During the Civil War, she worked with slaves who had been left behind when their owners joined the Confederate Army.

By 1864, Harriet was exhausted, and she was experiencing frequent seizures due to an old head injury. She went to Auburn to rest and recuperate. William Seward, Lincoln's

Secretary of State, obtained property for Harriet when she moved to Auburn; they maintained their friendship until he died in 1872.

On March 10, 1913, Harriet died of pneumonia at the age of ninety-three. Harriet was truly the Moses of her people; she was also an abolitionist, a humanitarian, a nurse, and a spy for the Union Army. Principally, she is remembered for her underground railroad activities, about which she said: "I never ran my train off the track, and I never lost a passenger."

GERRIT SMITH

Gerrit Smith of Peterboro, who was an organizer in the anti-slavery movement, was also active in the underground railroad. In *A Short History of New York State*, David M. Ellis, et al., comment that: "Probably the most irrepressible reformer was Gerrit Smith, whose career, like a seismograph, registered every tremor of the reform movement. Smith became interested in the benevolent societies.... Soon, he branched out into temperance and abolition, the major concern of his adult life.... He backed the crusade for women's rights."[11]

In addition to being a stationmaster on the underground railroad, Smith helped slaves purchase their freedom. On many occasions, escaped slaves stayed at Smith's home—the Peterboro underground railroad station—before being sent on their way to Canada. Smith supported the underground railroad movement until the traffic in slaves tapered off with the outbreak of the Civil War in 1861.

FREDERICK DOUGLASS

Frederick Douglass was an active conductor on the underground railroad in Rochester. He hid hundreds of escaping slaves at the *North Star* printing office and at his home. Eleven fugitives were the most that Douglass had under his roof. He had difficulty in providing so many at one time with food and shelter. He had to house and feed them until he could raise the money to transport them to Canada. He was thankful that they were contented with plain food and with a piece of carpet on the floor on which to sleep or a place in the hay-

Frederick Douglass

loft.

J. P. Morris was one of Douglass's main assistants in raising funds for the fugitives' escape. William S. Falls, production foreman for the Rochester *Daily Democrat*, was another principal aide. Falls hid slaves in his press room, which was on another floor of the same building that housed the *North Star* printing office. Falls solicited money for underground railroad efforts from downtown Rochester businesses.

Douglass also supported the women's rights movement. On July 14, 1848, his *North Star* carried this announcement: "A Convention to discuss the Social, Civil, and Religious Condition and Rights of Women will be held in the Wesleyan Chapel at Seneca Falls, New York, the 19th and 20th of July instant." The masthead that Douglass used for the *North Star* was: "RIGHT IS OF NO SEX—TRUTH IS OF NO COLOR."

Women's Rights Movement

In 1840, Lucretia Mott accompanied her husband, James, to London to the World Anti-Slavery Convention, where she met Elizabeth Cady Stanton. Women were denied seating as candidates to the convention. Lucretia and Elizabeth were relegated to the gallery with the other women to observe the activities of the convention, not to participate in them. They agreed to have a meeting to address women's issues when they returned to the United States. The meeting that Lucretia Mott and Elizabeth Cady Stanton had planned in London in 1840 finally occurred eight years later.

In early July 1848, Lucretia Mott visited her sister, Martha Wright, in Auburn and attended the yearly meeting of the Friends [Quakers] in western New York. Lucretia contacted Elizabeth Cady Stanton in Seneca Falls, and they decided to continue the discussion of women's rights begun in London.

Jane Hunt invited them to tea along with her friends, Martha Wright and Mary Ann M'Clintock. The five women discussed their frustration with the limited rights of women and the discrimination they had experienced in the temperance and antislavery movements.

Planning the first women's rights convention was done at the home of Jane and Richard Hunt in Waterloo. The women prepared a notice about the convention that appeared in the Seneca County *Courier* on July 14. They agreed to reconvene at the home of Mary Ann and Thomas M'Clintock in Waterloo on July 16 to prepare an agenda for the convention to be held in Seneca Falls on July 19-20.

At their meeting on July 16, the five women decided to list their grievances and to propose resolutions for them. The women asked Elizabeth Cady Stanton to write a *Declaration of Sentiments* patterned on the *Declaration of Independence*. She wanted the right to vote to be one of the resolutions. The other women wanted to emphasize other women's rights first and postpone the right-to-vote issue as being too controversial. Elizabeth Cady Stanton prevailed, and the controversial right of women to vote became one of the resolutions.

On July 19, James Mott called the convention to order in the Wesleyan Chapel. Lucretia Mott stated the goals of the convention and discussed the importance of educating women and elevating their social position. Mary Ann M'Clintock and Elizabeth Cady Stanton read prepared speeches, and Martha Wright read newspaper articles that she had written about the plight of women.

After the *Declaration of Sentiments* was discussed, it was reread by Elizabeth Cady Stanton and adopted with some minor amendments. The only resolution that was not unanimously adopted was the ninth, which concerned the right of women to vote. Some attendees of the convention thought that advancing the elective franchise of women at that time might reduce the probability of securing other rights for women. Because of Elizabeth Cady Stanton's continued support, the ninth resolution eventually passed with a slight majority.

• • •

Many activists worked for more than one reform movement. Theodore Weld was active in the antislavery and women's rights movements. Wendell Phillips, a New Englander, was a leader in the temperance and antislavery movements, as were Arthur and Lewis Tappan of New York City. Gerrit Smith was a force in the temperance and antislavery movements and supported the women's rights movement. Henry Stanton, Elizabeth Cady Stanton's husband, worked with Smith in the antislavery movement and aided his wife in her work in the women's rights movement.

Lucretia Mott, Elizabeth Cady Stanton, Susan B. Anthony, Amelia Bloomer, and Antoinette Brown were active in the temperance and women's rights movements. Cady Stanton wrote for Bloomer's temperance publication, *The Lily*. Frederick Douglass gave lectures on abolitionism and supported the women's rights movement, particularly in its early days.

The women's rights leaders supported Douglass in his effort to obtain the vote for African Americans. Obviously, the region was a focal point for reform activity. In *A Short History of New York State*, David M. Ellis, et al., observe that: "In this reform movement New York, particularly the upstate region, led the nation. No other section produced more leaders of the caliber of Theodore Weld, Charles Finney, Elizabeth Cady Stanton, Gerrit Smith, and the Tappan brothers of New York City."[12]

Thomas Lake Harris Mansion, Brocton

CHAPTER 1

Thomas Harris and the Brotherhood of the New Life

"The Christian Era has produced no more extraordinary seer and mystic than Thomas Lake Harris; yet, notwithstanding his remarkable occult powers, he is but little known outside the circle of his friends and disciples. His range of clairvoyant vision, if we may judge by what he has written, was so extensive that it not only embraced our Solar System, but extended far beyond its outermost limits. He also claimed to have been in conscious touch with the great Adepts of the old Gold and Silver Ages of the remote past. He is mainly known to the comparatively few who have known him through his connection with Laurence Oliphant, and as the founder of the Brotherhood of the New Life.... Whatever else he may have been he was unquestionably one of the greatest seers of modern times; also a philosopher who propounded a wonderfully comprehensive system of Christian philosophy, embracing not only a religious and ethical, but also a social and economic aspect. He is perhaps best defined as a Theo-socialist."[13]

W.P. Swainson, *Thomas Lake Harris and His Occult Teaching*

Thomas Harris and the Brotherhood of the New Life

The Brotherhood of the New Life was similar to other nine-teenth century groups that espoused mysticism, in that it represented an abandonment of existing religions to establish a theocratic society based on viewpoints expressed in collections of myths about sex. In the opinion of Herbert W. Schneider and George Lawton in *A Prophet and a Pilgrim*:

> The history of our country is filled with instances of small bands of idealistic men and women who, having rejected the main ethical, religious, and economic codes of their day, have followed a prophet out into the wilderness to hew out in peace and privacy an existence close to their dreams. Of such intrepid but doomed groups, the Brotherhood of the New Life was one of the most curious and relatively successful. It was successful in making a living because its members cooperated intelligently and industriously in the business. Harris was apparently a shrewd manager and the Oliphants [the pilgrim and his mother] and their friends furnished much of the necessary capital....
>
> No utopia ever had a more ambitious ideology. This family, or brotherhood, was to be the earthly home of God's regenerating breath, the matrix of world redemption. It was the "pivotal" center on earth of "arch-natural" society, that is, of society in which human and celestial beings unite. As crisis after crisis of world judgment arose, it appeared to the prophet and "primate" of this society that it alone would survive the general catastrophe.[14]

Early Life

Thomas Lake Harris was born on May 15, 1823, in Fenny Stratford, England, to Thomas Harris and Annie Lake Harris. The family immigrated to the United States in 1828. Thomas Harris, Sr., was an auctioneer in Utica, where he also owned and managed a grocery store. He believed in the teachings of Calvin and was a deacon in the Baptist Church.

Annie Lake Harris died when Thomas Lake was nine, and his father remarried soon after her death. Young Thomas, who had been extremely close to his mother, did not get along with his stepmother. He earned money from part-time jobs and became somewhat independent of his family. He spent much of his time thinking about God and remembering his mother. His interest in poetry began at a young age. He joined the Universalist Church and by the age of eighteen considered himself a sinner.

As a young man, Harris was quiet, unassuming, and in somewhat delicate health. However, he was lively, and his animated conversation was considered brilliant. He possessed a notable ability to improvise. He could extemporaneously compose poetry, and he gradually evolved into a motivational speaker.

According to Richard M'Cully in *The Brotherhood of the New Life and Thomas Harris*, at the age of eighteen Harris experienced an epiphany upon his return from an autumn walk. His room was "illuminated with a soft moonlight radiance, full of the sparkles of invisible gems." His mother appeared to him in "waving, floating, coruscating" light, placed her hand on his forehead, and uttered "a speech which flowed into expression in the soul."

In 1845, Harris married Mary Van Arnum and became the minister of the Fourth Universalist Society in New York City. In the two years that Harris and his wife lived there, he was influenced by Spiritualist Andrew Jackson Davis and became a practicing medium. Davis believed that Father-God (Love) was joined with Mother-Nature (Substance) and arrived at "nuptial law" (Association). Harris dissociated himself from Davis when Davis began to advocate free love.

Harris was a prolific writer. In *An Epic of the Starry Heavens*, he describes an experience that he had in March 1850:

> Having entered my room, I became first of all conscious of a soft white luster, different at once from the ordinary gas-light and from the solar ray ... I was now impressed to look up, and saw, without any astonishment or without losing in any degree this delightful calmness, a tall and majestic Spirit, apparently in the perfection of manhood....

> This Spirit stood before me holding in his right hand a small book, which appeared to be bound in the ancient Gothic style and clasped with a seven-fold seal. Without saying a word, he proceeded to open the book, which I at once perceived from its peculiar appearance to be a depository of divine truth and wisdom....

> While I was contemplating the picture, the Angel spoke in a voice full of expression and said: "Do you perceive that all the knowledge which hitherto you have attained to, is far exceeded by the wisdom contained in the first and most minute of the hieroglyphs?" The effect of his address was to produce a more interior illumination of intellect, and I perceived and at once answered in the affirmative.

> At this the Angel smiled in a serious way and said, with increased and even with paternal

gentleness. "Be faithful and obedient, and in
four years this volume all shall be opened to
you." Saying this he closed the book and
became invisible.[15]

Shortly after this experience, Harris's wife died. She had
given birth to two sons and may have died giving birth to a
third child. Having been deeply in love with her and much
grieved by her death, he dedicated *An Epic of the Starry
Heavens* to her in 1853 and referred to her in *Regina*, which
he wrote in 1859. His *Song of Theos* provides us with a representative sample of his poetry:

At last comes "Spiritism" misconceived;
In selfhood reasoned, Christlessly believed,
Held in the proud conception of self's thought;
The "god of this world" whereof Christus taught;
The god who in degeneration grows,
And is degeneration to its close.

Behold your god, O peoples, ye who swim
In the self vortex. Yield your fates to him.
He asks no martyrdoms; he gives you fees
Of fond self-praises; mutual flatteries.
He tints Elysium on the selfhood's eyen.
"Take ye the world. See all thereof is mine,
And I bestow it unto those I will—
I, self, incarnate in you, am you still."[16]

Following the death of his wife, Harris joined a group that
founded a spiritualist agricultural community in Mountain
Cove, West Virginia, where it was reported that they awaited
the Second Coming of Christ. Harris edited the community
newspaper, *The Mountain Cove Journal*, and he functioned as
a "medium" providing direction for the community. The
community lasted for only two years; the residents couldn't

agree on communal ownership of the property.

Harris returned to New York, where, in 1854, he wrote *Lyric*, in which he described his spiritual marriage to Queen Lily of the Conjugal Angels. In the following year, he married Emily Isabella Waters, who recognized the Lily Queen as her husband's true mate. They practiced celibacy for the entire thirty years of their marriage.

The Middle Years

In 1855, Harris became a Swedenborgian minister. Christian spiritualism as espoused by Emanuel Swedenborg, the Swedish scientist, philosopher, and theologian, was popular during the 1850s. In middle age, Swedenborg left the field of scientific research to inquire into psychical and spiritual subjects.

In his later years, he wrote that he left the natural sciences "when heaven was opened to him." Even before this revelation, he had visions and heard conversations that influenced his move away from science. He wrote extensively on the interpretation of the Scriptures.

Swedenborg did not try to found a sect. He believed that members of all church denominations could belong to his Church of the New Jerusalem (New Church) without establishing a separate organization. In New York City, two liberal groups existed within the New Church: a group of radical thinkers that included Henry James, Sr., who was influenced by François Fourier and Robert Owen, and a more spiritualistic group represented by Professor George Bush of New York University. Harris became a leader of Professor Bush's group. Harris founded the New Church Publishing Association and published *The Herald of Light*.

Swedenborg advocated three degrees of being. He agreed with the dualism of spirit described by Descartes but added a third degree, the celestial world. Swedenborg considered celestial being the inner union of spiritual beings. He did not believe in the concept of Christian redemption. Harris began to move away from Swedenborgianism to go his own way and to write prolifically about his beliefs.

Sexual mysticism was a favorite topic for Harris. He attempted to explain his view of spiritual marriage in *Arcana of Christianity*:

> The Eternal Masculinity is the Divine Love. The Eternal Femininity is the Divine Truth. The eternal proceeding of the two is the Divine Ability. The mystery of the Divine Nature is typified in the relations of conjugal love. In conjugal order, upon the orderly earths of the universe, the husband takes his wife to his bosom and they are at-one, the external expression being the nuptial rite, never to be identified with aught that is unchaste.

> In the nuptial blending of an angelic spouse with his companion, there is an interblending of spirit with spirit, until the wife is absorbed into the being of the husband, with all her faculties and powers folded up within his faculties and powers.... When they have attained to this condition they typify and represent the Lord. In Him the Eternal Masculine and the Eternal Feminine, otherwise Divine Good and Divine Truth, are one, forevermore, in the Holy Ghost.[17]

In 1859, Harris accepted an invitation to preach in England, where he stayed for two years. He continued to be very productive in his writing. While in England, Harris met Laurence Oliphant, who was to become the most prominent member of the Brotherhood of the New Life for many years.

In 1861, Harris settled with the Brotherhood of the New Life in Wassaic, Dutchess County. Long-term members of the

Brotherhood, Miss Jane Lee Waring and Mr. and Mrs. James A. Requa followed him from New York City. Two years later, the Brotherhood moved to a larger site in nearby Amenia, where they bought a grist mill and established a bank with Requa as cashier.

The community became known as the "Use." All members were expected to be influenced by the Divine Use. They practiced "open breathing," a manner of respiration in which the Divine Breath, the Holy Spirit, entered into the body. Harris taught that Adam-Eve was created in the Divine image, masculine-feminine, which he referred to as Twain-One, just as the Divine Jesus-Yessa or Christus-Christa was Twain-One also. Harris believed that each person lived in spiritual union with his or her heavenly "counterpart," as he did with his Queen Lily of the Conjugal Angels. He also believed that in heaven all men and women would attain union with God, and that "conjugal spirits" would be joined in perfect unity.

The Pilgrim

Laurence Oliphant and his mother, Lady Oliphant, joined the Brotherhood in Amenia. Laurence's father, Anthony Oliphant, was a barrister who had served as Attorney General of the Cape of Good Hope and as Chief Justice of Ceylon. He was knighted in 1839. In his youth, Laurence was very close to his mother. He was known for his sense of humor, his sincerity, and his positive attitude. In his later years, he was considered a person whom one could trust. People would open up to him even if they didn't know him well.

Young Oliphant followed in his father's footsteps and studied law at Lincoln's Inn in London. He enjoyed writing and began to write travel articles for *Blackwood's Magazine* and books about his travels. The first of his many travel books was *A Journey to Katmandu* in 1852. While in India, he became interested in mesmerism.

Oliphant became the private secretary to Lord Elgin, Governor General of Canada, and moved in the highest social circles in England. He held a number of diplomatic posts and eventually became England's first minister to Japan. Upon his return to England, he was elected to Parliament. However, Oliphant was not happy with his life. Biographer Margaret Oliphant described her cousin at this time: "It was very difficult to realize how a man so apparently successful in everything he touched should be possessed with so strong a sense of dissatisfaction, so much impatience and indignation, with his present mode of life."[18]

Oliphant applied for admission to the Brotherhood while they were located in Wassaic, but Harris made him consider his decision more deeply. He told Oliphant that if he were ultimately accepted, he would be be put through a humbling experience, such as performing menial tasks. Oliphant's London friends could not understand his decision to consider a life of hardship in a backwoods American religious community. Lady Oliphant had joined the Brotherhood two years before her son joined; her period of probation was less rigorous and lengthy than her son's.

Oliphant lived in isolation when he first joined the Brotherhood and eventually did farm chores. He turned over $90,000 to $100,000 to Harris, which became community property. Oliphant described his experiences in the Use in a letter to a friend:

> I have found in doing this kind of work, that we must trust to Divine guidance in every step. Success is certain if we do, but if we venture upon a single move in the selfhood, failure is inevitable. This has been several times proved to me by bitter experience, and yet I cannot practice it. In the most minute details of life, such as the varied incidents in my life as a teamster, I find that the only escape from a difficulty is by asking God to help me out of it, and when my state is not good everything is

certain to go wrong. The evil ones have you at a disadvantage and results become instantly apparent. When one is working directly in the Lord's service, the responsibility becomes awful, and in fact should only be undertaken after the most earnest prayer, and in a most solemn frame of mind....[19]

Relocation of the Brotherhood to Brocton

In 1867, Harris moved the Brotherhood to a 1,600-acre site called Salem-on-Erie, near Dunkirk on Lake Erie. It was a much larger site than Amenia with room for expansion. He was financially aided by Lady Oliphant in purchasing the site. Buffalo newspaper journalist Willard E. Keyes later observed that "the rich valleys and sunny hillsides of central and western New York have always had strong attractions for religious and socialistic colonies."[20] The community engaged in farming and grape growing; it evolved from being a quasi-communistic settlement to a patriarchal society with Harris, the "father," controlling and administering the jointly held property.

Members of the Use, about forty, were all devout Christians. Baptists were the principal denomination. One member was a Quaker and four were Shakers. Every member worked. The Use planted extensive vineyards, including fifteen acres of the Salem grape variety. They built a massive below-ground wine vault, 100 feet long and 18 feet wide, of solid masonry. Initially, they produced 15,000 gallons of wine annually.

Outsiders were not sure how to describe the Use. In religious terms, Harris did not consider the Use to be a cult. His view of the Brotherhood's social relations was:

Personally, I am not a Communist.... We are Socialists, believing in the association of noble and cultivated souls for every industrial and human service.... In the present state of society in the United States, no pure communism can succeed. Our people are too strongly individual. If you remove from the members of any community the spur of individual necessity and reward you have a community of partial non-producers.[21]

Oliphant expanded upon that viewpoint:

It is an entire misnomer to speak of us as a community. We have no communism among us. We are simply a band of persons, who thinking alike on most subjects, having a strong democratic tendency, holding enthusiastically the same religious views, and being equally desirous of doing God's will and making our daily lives one continuous act of obedience to his command—in fact, making every day a Sunday—have associated ourselves together and live together, hoping that while by the concentration of our energies and by mutual religious sustainment we may benefit ourselves both here and hereafter. We may, at the same time set a lively example to others, and, if we cannot draw them to ourselves, lead them to do as we do in other places.[22]

At Brocton the sexes were not segregated, nor did Harris consider segregation necessary. The rumor that the Use condoned lax sexual morals like some other communities was dispelled by Robert Martin, one of the Brotherhood's most strict members: "Nothing could have been further from the truth. If ever there was a strait-laced, God-fearing band of men and women, it was the first little handful of earnest souls who were led to believe that they, under the guidance of

Harris, were to lead the world into the land where there was neither sin nor sorrow, neither from suffering nor death."[23]

Harris required members to practice celibacy until they were "free from lust." Some marriages were permitted. Harris believed that some people were more able, after marriage, to ward off "infestation" or the "approach of psychic sex."

Harris remodeled the farmhouse at Brocton, expanded it to thirty rooms, and named it Vine Cliff. It was the largest house in the Use and, in fact, in Brocton. He planted shrubs and trees so that the house was not visible from the nearby highway. Miss Waring was in charge of the landscaping. In Robert Martin's opinion, "When those wonderful gardens were abloom, there was nothing in the surrounding country to compare with it."

The Move to California and Schism

In 1875, Harris moved the Use to Santa Rosa, California, where he purchased a 1,200-acre vineyard on a site called Fountain Grove. Harris and others had grown tired of the severe winters on the shores of Lake Erie. The Santa Rosa enterprise produced 15,000 to 20,000 gallons of wine annually and was aided by gifts from abroad; however, the California site was not as prosperous as Salem-on-Erie.

Harris perceived the Santa Rosa Use as the focal point for the regeneration of mankind. He started a new publication, a collection of essays, poems, and revelations, similar to the *Herald of Light* that he had published earlier but with the goal of increasing membership. Harris summarized much of this material in his book, *The Lord: The Two-in-One*. The publication, which was free, was used to disseminate his principles. For the first time, he actively recruited converts.

In 1870, Oliphant returned to England. Apparently, Harris had suggested that Oliphant leave the community for a period of time. Oliphant became a tailor upon his return to England. After all, he had gained experience in the Use in sewing clothing and in hemming towels. Oliphant, who paid a London tailor £500 to teach him how to make coats and trousers, sent his earnings to Brocton. However, Oliphant soon decided that he was better suited to his old profession, journalism. He reported on the Franco-Prussian War for the London *Times*.

In the following year in Paris, Oliphant met and fell in love with Alice Le Strange, a beautiful, talented woman, who was willing to accept his religious views. Alice agreed to go to Brocton to meet Harris and to join the Brotherhood. In 1872, Laurence Oliphant and Alice Le Strange were married in London. It is not clear whether Harris gave his blessing to the union. He may have specified that they were not to live together as man and wife. Oliphant verified the agreement: "I learnt self-control by sleeping with my beloved and beautiful Alice in my arms for twelve years without claiming the rights of a husband. We lived as sister and brother. I am a passionate lover, and so it was difficult, very difficult.... But it did not prove to be impossible. I was able to keep my vow, and I shall never regret having made it."[24]

In 1875, the year of the move to California, Oliphant began to distance himself from Harris. In 1881, he broke completely with Harris, who later returned the money that Oliphant had turned over to the Brotherhood when he joined. This triggered other members to ask for the money that they had contributed to the Brotherhood. These financial concerns and the fact that Oliphant stayed in contact with the community at Brocton caused turmoil that some members referred to as the schism.

In 1886, Alice Le Strange Oliphant died of a fever that she had contracted on her world travels with her husband. Oliphant returned to England where he continued his writing, including a novel, light satire, a travel book, and autobiographical material.

The Later Years
In his later years, Harris moved beyond Christian and Jewish theology toward Oriental religion and philosophy, although

he had not studied Eastern thought. He seemed to be evolving from prophet to avatar, an incarnation or embodiment of a concept. In Hindu philosophy, an avatar is the incarnation of a deity in human form.

In *Declarations*, Harris expanded upon his concept of the Divine Mother:

> "My Mother, I am in love toward you as if you were the Divine Woman of my soul, and the Life of its delights." The Mother answered, "I love My babe; the child, in the womb of My Chaste Maternity, is enfolded in bridal endearments, by which it was first begun, and in which it is continually being ministered to, and unfolded toward completeness. As a babe, you are now enfolded in My Greater Personality; and I am communicating to you, whom I hold enwombed, My greater personality of a greater space."[25]

To Harris, this return to the Divine Mother's womb represented the apex of spiritual joy. He was now moving toward the Hindu concept of the Divine Mother.

Harris's second wife, Emily Isabella Waters, died in 1885. In 1891, he married Jane Lee Waring, a prominent member of the Use. They traveled to England and, upon their return, settled in New York City. He continued to write and to insist that he had not founded a cult. Harris died in New York City on March 23, 1906.

In 1906, at the time of his death, Harris's followers numbered 2,000, including Harrisites in England and Scotland. Harris's long-term associate and biographer Arthur Cuthbert (*The Life and World-Work of Thomas Lake Harris*) tried to keep the Brotherhood together, but Cuthbert did not have Harris's strong leadership qualities. When Cuthbert died on March 25, 1914, Mrs. Harris attempted to provide continuity within the Brotherhood, but she was unable to sustain the community.

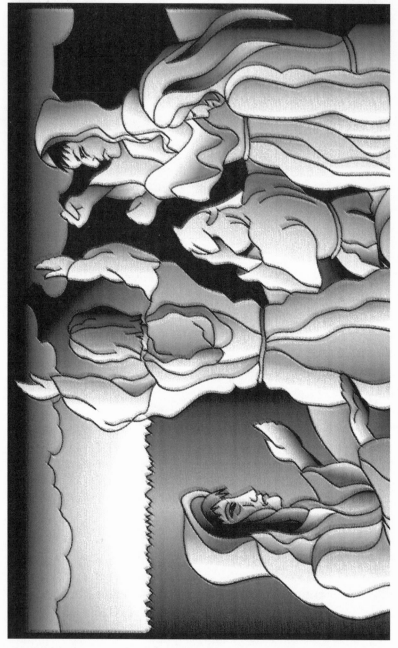

Millerites on Cobbs Hill, Rochester

CHAPTER 2

William Miller and the Millerites

"In the Apocryhpha, the end of the world was generally held to be predicted to occur in 1,000 years, with different theories as to what constituted a 'year.' The Last Judgment was expected by many in 999, but it did not happen. Since then, prophets of doom and Apocalypse have frequently predicted the end of the world. No man in America created more havoc predicting the Second Coming of Christ than did a former atheist turned fire-and-brimstoner named William Miller. A New York farmer, Miller—by diligent, if mysterious, biblical research in the Books of Daniel and Revelation—determined the end of the world would occur on April 23, 1843.

The fanatical Miller had an overpowering personality and not only gathered a devoted cult around him but even convinced the New York *Herald* to take him seriously; it printed his prediction of the great fire that would envelop the earth. He was convinced that Napoleon had been visited on humanity as the Anti-Christ heralding the onrushing Last Judgment. Miller arrived at this conclusion in 1831; he found confirmation of his premise in a shower of shooting stars in 1833; a great comet, the brightest of the century, gave conclusive confirmation in March 1843."[26]

Carl Sifakis, *American Eccentrics*

William Miller—Predictor of the End of the World

During the first half of the nineteenth century, William Miller, a farmer-soldier-preacher from the New York-Vermont border, studied prophecies and concluded that the Apocalypse was going to occur within his lifetime. He went on the road preaching his version of evangelism. His followers were called Millerites and Adventists. Miller's preaching appealed to members of many religious denominations, including Baptists, Methodists, and Presbyterians. His followers, estimated to be from 10,000 to one million, tended to retain their membership in their Protestant churches in addition to believing in Millerism.

When pressured by a colleague to predict a date for the end of the world, initially Miller predicted April 23, 1843. When the sun came up that day, he changed his prediction to October 22, 1844. In his book, *Thunder and Trumpets*, David L. Rowe describes the event:

> On October 22, 1844, hundreds of New Yorkers throughout the State watched the skies expectantly for the Second Coming of Christ. A scoffing public called these people Millerites for William Miller, the Low Hampton, New York, farmer who had sparked this excitement with his lectures on the approaching end of the world. But they called themselves adventists, often capitalizing the label to brandish before unbelievers their self-conscious identity as people who were separate from other professing Christians, superior to them in faith and understanding of the Bible.
>
> Like other "watchers on the walls of Zion" in New England, Pennsylvania, Canada, Ohio, and the farther west, they believed that at any

moment the Son of Man would descend to earth from Heaven through clouds ablaze with lightning and reverberating with the crash of thunder and the compelling call of celestial trumpets. Then, an enraged God would would shower purifying fire upon the corrupt earth, shatter cities and topple thrones with earthquakes, put an end to the reign of churches and governments, and send the wicked to the punishment they deserved. Only true Christians, those who were now watching for His coming, praying for it, yearning for the rewards Christ would mete out to the saints, were to taste the joys of paradise in the New Jerusalem.[27]

William Miller was born on a farm in Pittsfield, Massachusetts, on February 15, 1782. Four years later, the family moved to Low Hampton, New York, near the Vermont State line. He grew up in a Baptist family. His mother was very religious. As the oldest of sixteen children, he was no stranger to farm work and household chores. As a young child, he read history, fiction, and poetry whenever he could. The family had little money to spend on books.

On June 30, 1803, Miller married Lucy Smith of Poultney, Vermont, and moved to his wife's hometown. He joined the Masons, was appointed Constable, and, in 1809, became Deputy Sheriff. In 1810, he was commissioned lieutenant in the Vermont militia. He continued to be a deeply religious person, influenced by his grandfather, Elnathan Phelps, pastor of the Baptist church at Orwell, and his uncle, Elihu Miller, pastor of the Baptist church at Low Hampton.

During the War of 1812, Miller had strong patriotic feelings. In 1813, he was commissioned lieutenant in the U.S. Army and, within two years, was promoted to captain. In 1814, he participated in the Battle of Prattsburgh, which the Americans won even though they were outmanned by the

British Army and by the Royal Navy on the Hudson River. Miller retired from the Army in June 1815 and returned to Poultney to resume his work on the farm. Within a short time, he moved back to Low Hampton.

Miller Becomes Interested in Prophecies

Upon leaving the Army, Miller became a more religious person. Despite the patriotic feelings he had experienced earlier, he questioned his participation in the War of 1812. He spent his spare time reading the Bible. Miller realized that something was missing; he was not at peace with himself. He searched for additional meaning for his life. Ultimately, he reached a point of epiphany, as recorded in his journal:

> Suddenly the character of a Savior was vividly impressed upon my mind. It seemed that there might be a Being so good and compassionate as to Himself atone for our transgressions, and thereby save us from suffering the penalty of sin. I immediately felt how lovely such a Being must be; and imagined that I could cast myself into the arms of, and trust in the mercy of, such a One....

> I felt that to believe in such a Savior without evidence, would be visionary in the extreme. I saw that the Bible did bring to view just such a Savior as I needed; and I was perplexed to find how an uninspired book should develop principles so perfectly adapted to the wants of a fallen world. I was constrained to admit that the Scriptures must be a revelation from God; they became my delight, and in Jesus I found a friend.[28]

For over fourteen years, Miller divided his time between

farming and studying the Bible. He noted that the prophecies in the Bible about the First Advent of Christ had obviously been fulfilled. He concluded that the prophecies that had been fulfilled in the past should provide some enlightenment on future events. He reasoned that the Second Advent of Christ should be anticipated.

In particular, he read and reread the Book of Revelation and the prophecies of Daniel, particularly the declaration, "Unto two thousand and three hundred days, then the sanctuary be cleansed." He began to think about the timing of the Second Coming of Christ followed by the destruction of the earth by fire.

Miller felt that he should speak out on his observations about the Second Advent:

> The duty of presenting the evidence of the nearness of the Advent to others—which I had managed to evade while I found the shadow of an objection remaining against the truth— again came home to me with great force. I had previously only thrown out occasional hints of my views. I then began to speak more clearly to my neighbors, to ministers, and others. To my astonishment, I found very few who listened with any interest. Occasionally, one would see the force of the evidence, but the great majority passed it by as an idle tale.[29]

Miller was a serious man who had spent many years studying the issues of the Second Coming. Initially, the prospect of preaching his thoughts on the subject did not occur to him. After all, he was not an ordained minister. One day he was calculating the timing of the Second Awakening based on the Jewish calendar, when he thought he heard a voice say, "Go tell it to the world."

Early in 1833, the Baptist church in Low Hampton had no

minister, and Miller was asked to preach. On September 14, 1833, the Baptist church gave him a license to preach. Shortly after he began preaching, certain natural phenomenon seemed to support his discussions about the Second Coming and the end of the world.

On November 13, 1833, thousands of stars fell to the earth. The shooting stars were documented in "Last Day Tokens," published in 1843. Miller and his followers interpreted these celestial fireworks as support for his prophecies. His following continued to grow. He branched out from small villages and towns and began to preach in large cities.

Rev. Joshua V. Himes Helps Miller Promote His Prophecies

In November 1840, Miller received an invitation from the Rev. Joshua V. Himes to preach in the Chardon Street Chapel in Boston. Himes attended all of Miller's lectures and was deeply moved by what he heard. Himes observed, "I laid myself, family, society, reputation, all, upon the altar of God, to help him, to the extent of my power, to the end."[30] Himes was an active individual whose real strength was promotion.

Initially, Himes had difficulty believing that the world was going to be destroyed, possibly in 1843 as Miller had been suggesting. In his early association with Miller, Himes noted that Miller's prophecies could be used to increase religious enthusiasm. Himes envisioned motivating people to show concern for their sins and to seek repentance. Eventually, Himes truly believed Miller's prophecies, and he began to use his considerable promotional abilities to spread the word.

As soon as Himes had ascertained the depth and strength of Miller's beliefs, he asked him what he was doing to alert the public about his prophecies. Himes knew that the movement needed its own publication to publicize Miller's thinking. In 1840, he began to publish *Signs of the Times,* which he renamed *The Advent Herald* four years later.

The editor of the Maine *Wesleyan Journal* reported his

observations about Miller and his lectures:

> Mr. Miller is a great stickler for literal inter-
> pretations; never admitting the figurative,
> unless absolutely required to make correct
> sense or meet the event which is to be pointed
> out. He doubtless believes, most unwavering-
> ly, all he teaches to others. His lectures are
> interspersed with powerful admonitions to the
> wicked....
>
> He is evidently disposed to make little
> allowance for those who think differently from
> him on the millennium; dealing often in terri-
> ble denunciations against such as oppose his
> peculiar views on this point; as he fully
> believes they are crying peace and safety when
> sudden destruction cometh. Judging from
> what we see and hear, we should think his lec-
> tures are making a decided impression on
> many minds, favorable to his theory.[31]

Elder Himes actively spread the word of the Millerites. He published "Memoir of William Miller," which includes some of his writings in addition to Miller's. Himes planned a series of lectures in New York City. Attendance at the early lectures was meager, but the concluding lectures in the series were presented to full halls.

Millerites held camp meetings in New England during the summer of 1842. The first large camp meeting in 1843 was held in Rochester. The big tent collapsed in the heavy winds of a rainstorm, but contributions from Miller faithful in the city allowed to tent to be repaired and erected again. Until the tent was repaired, meetings were held in the market, where several thousand people assembled. Brother Himes gave three sermons over a period of eight hours. He captured and retained the attention of the audience even though most of them had to stand. Many people came from the surrounding countryside to the location of the collapsed tent, were unable to find the meeting, and went home disappointed.

Although Rochester was considered the western outpost of the Millerite movement, camp meetings were also held in Buffalo and in Ohio. The promotional techniques of the movement were in evidence in Rochester. A paper, *The Glad Tidings*, was printed and distributed in the Genesee region and along the Erie Canal for thirteen weeks, and a bookstore that sold and gave away Millerite literature was opened.

Until 1843, Miller was imprecise about his prediction of the Second Coming. He usually said "about the year 1843" in referring to the event. On January 1, 1843, Miller refined his prediction in a statement of his beliefs, and in the January 1843 issue of *Signs of the Times*, Millerite leaders refuted a claim that they had set a specific day for the Second Coming:

> I believe the time can be known by all who desire to understand and to be ready for His coming. And I am fully convinced that sometime between March 21, 1843, and March 21, 1844, according to the Jewish mode of computation of time, Christ will come, and bring all His saints with Him; and that then He will reward every man as his work shall be....
>
> The fact is, that the believers of the Second Advent in 1843 have fixed no time in the year for the event. And Brethren Miller, Himes, Litch, Hale, Fitch, Hawley, and other prominent lecturers, most decidedly protest against ... fixing the day or hour of the event. This we have done over and over again, in our paper.[32]

In early 1843, a rumor circulated that the Millerites had

predicted that the end of the world would occur on April 23, 1843. The Millerites repeatedly denied that they had chosen this date. This rumor was spread widely, as far as South America.

Although the Millerites continued to attract followers, many others spoke out against the movement. Negative articles about Miller and his prophecies were published in Boston and Philadelphia. A newspaper article in Trenton, New Jersey, was particularly negative:

> Mr. Miller has been holding forth on his narrow-minded humbug at Trenton to large audiences.... This Miller does not appear to be a knave, but simply a fool, or more properly a monomaniac. If the Almighty intended to give due notice of the world's destruction, He would not do it by sending a fat, illiterate old fellow to preach bad grammar and worse sense, down in Jersey![33]

Miller was called many things, including a fool, a liar, and a zealot. A newspaper staffwriter referred to one of his meetings as a orgy. Those in attendance, however, commented on the serious, well-behaved nature of his followers.

Predicting the Date of the Second Coming

Miller personally hesitated to cite specific dates for the Second Coming; however, Elder Himes strongly suggested that Miller forecast the particular day on which the end of the world would occur. Similar to the speculation that accompanied the shooting star shower of 1833, the brightest comet of the century in March 1843 was viewed as a harbinger of things to come.

Miller's calculation of the date of the event was based on the 2,300 days of Daniel 8:14. He incorporated an interpretation like that used by Protestant commentators in which a day represented a year; he calculated the date in a number of different ways. In the first example, calculation starts with the date of the decree to rebuild Jerusalem, 457 BC (Daniel 9:25). By adding 2,300 years to that date, 1843 was the forecast date of the end of the world. A second calculation was made by adding the 1,335 days (years) mentioned in Daniel 12:12 to AD 508, when Papal supremacy was established, to arrive again at 1843.

A more complex computation involved additional elements, again with days representing years:

- Number of days from the decree to rebuild   490
  Jerusalem, 457 BC, to the crucifixion of
  Christ, 70 weeks, or 490 years

- Number of days from the crucifixion of Christ   475
  to taking away Pagan rites

- Number of days from taking away Pagan rites   30
  to the establishment of Papal civil rule

- Number of days from setting up Papal civil rule 1,260
  to its discontinuance

- Number of days from the discontinuance of   45
  Papal civil rule to the end of the world in 1843

Total number of years   2,300

A variation of this calculation begins with the establishment of Papal civil rule in AD 538 (sometimes considered to be AD 508) and incorporates additional elements. By adding the 1,260 days of the woman in the wilderness described in Revelation 12:14, the sum is 1,748, the date of the de-emphasis of the Papacy by the Emperor Napoleon. The 45 days needed to arrive at 1843 are then added as in the previous calculation. Another calculation was made by subtracting the 70 weeks (490 years) of Daniel 9:24 from the 2,300 days (years) and adding the life of Christ (33 years) to arrive at 1843.

The last example was based upon Leviticus XXVI: 23-24 in which the Lord discusses the punishment of Israel "yet seven times for their sins." Again with days considered to be years, seven times 360 days a year is 2,520 years. By subtracting the date of the first captivity in Babylon, 677 BC, when, supposedly, this punishment began, from 2,520, the end of the world was calculated to be in AD 1843.

The "Great Disappointment"

Miller claimed that the year 1843 actually went from March 21, 1843, to March 21, 1844, because the prophecies were based on the Jewish calendar, and the dates should be converted to conventional calendar dates. The date of the event selected by many Millerites was April 23, 1843. When the Second Coming did not occur on that date, a number of alternate dates were discussed within the movement; October 22, 1844, became the most frequently forecast date.

Most Millerites sincerely believed in this date. Farmers neglected to plant crops during the spring, and those who did plant crops left them unharvested. Other Millerites closed their businesses and gave away their money and household goods. Generally, they behaved as anti-Millerites expected people who believed in the coming of the millennium to behave.

As the prophesied day approached, many of the faithful gathered in homes or in churches. Millerites in Philadelphia left the city to camp out in the country. Miller stood on a large, flat rock near his home while viewing the New England scenery and waiting for the cataclysm that did not occur. One of the many stories that circulated about the Millerites was that they wore long, flowing, white muslin robes early in the morning on what they perceived to be their last day.

In Rochester, observers claimed that Millerites wore

ascension robes while standing on Cobb's Hill, one of the highest elevations in Rochester, waiting for the sun NOT to come up. Generally, these robe stories were denied by the Millerites; however, at least one incident of the wearing of robes was documented (in Haverhill, Massachusetts).

In the first edition of the Millerite publication *The Midnight Cry*, Elder Himes wrote an editorial entitled "Provision for the Destitute:"

> As many of our brethren and sisters have disposed of their substance, and given alms, agreeable to Luke 12:33, in the confident expectation of the speedy coming of the Lord, I wish to have immediate provision made for the comforts and wants of all such persons and families by the advent brethren. We must not permit them to be dependent upon the world, or that portion of the professed church who scoff at our hope. We hope no application will be made to such for aid in this work of charity....
>
> Let committees of faithful and judicious men be raised in every city and town to whom contributions may be given for the poor saints.... Some among us still have this world's goods and can render present aid to the destitute. I doubt not all will do their duty.[34]

Following the second of their disappointments, Millerites were the target of considerable verbal abuse in the press, including accusations of financial irresponsibility. Miller stated his feelings in a letter to Himes:

> Although I have been twice disappointed, I am not cast down or discouraged. God has been

with me in spirit and has comforted me. I have now much more evidence that I do believe in God's Word; and although surrounded with enemies and scoffers, yet my mind is perfectly calm, and my hope in the coming of Christ is as strong as ever. I have done only what after years of sober consideration I felt to be my solemn duty to do.

If I have erred, it has been on the side of charity, the love of my fellow man, and my conviction of duty to God.... I had not a distant thought of disturbing our churches, ministers, or religious editors, or departing from the best Biblical commentaries or rules which had been recommended for the study of the Scriptures.[35]

An advent conference held at Low Hampton in late December was the last significant event for the Millerites in 1844. Conference attendees asked Miller to prepare an "Address to Advent Believers," to help them understand the miscalculation that caused their great disappointment. Miller attempted to explain:

The discrepancy, we believe, is in the human part of chronology, and as there are four or five years in dispute among our best chronological writers, which cannot be satisfactorily settled, we feel that we have a good right to this disputed period; and candid and reasonable men will all allow this to be right. Therefore we must patiently wait the time in dispute before we can honestly confess we are wrong in time.[36]

The Millerite movement collapsed following the "Great Disappointment" and split into three factions:

> The largest body, which included Miller and other prominent leaders, admitted their incorrect chronology but continued to expect the imminent end of the world; they later took the name Advent Christians. A much smaller group, sometimes called the "spiritualizers," insisted that the Second Advent had actually occurred—in a spiritual sense—on October 22, but within a short time many of these ex-Millerites had joined other religious movements such as the Shakers. A third faction, the future Seventh-day Adventists, rationalized that Christ had entered the "most holy place" of a "heavenly sanctuary" on October 22 and that he would soon return to earth.[37]

One of the last gatherings of Millerites was held in Albany in the spring of 1845 in an attempt to keep the movement united. The conference was perceived as a stabilizing influence for Adventists.

The Later Years of Miller and Himes

In early 1848, Miller's eyesight began to fail and his general health declined. He died on December 20, 1849, at his home in Low Hampton. Elder Himes, who had worked hard to promote his views and to publish his thoughts, was at his side when he died. Miller was buried in a graveyard near his home. Two lines are carved into his tombstone, one above his name and one below: "At the time appointed the end shall be" and "But go thy way until the end shall be: for thou shalt rest and stand in thy lot at the end of the days."

After subscribing to Millerism for over thirty years, Elder Himes renounced his beliefs. In January 9, 1880, Himes was ordained a minister in the Episcopal Church by Bishop Clarkson of Nebraska and assigned to St. Andrew's Church in Elk Point, South Dakota. The 1,081 inhabitants of Elk Point knew little of Himes's experience as a leader in the Millerite movement. He was active in the Episcopal Church until his death on July 27, 1895.

Adventism after the Millerites

Several Adventist movements grew out of the Millerite movement. On November 6, 1861, the Advent Christian Church was founded in Worcester, Massachusetts. The Church is similar to other Protestant denominations. Obviously, one of its distinguishing characteristics is its emphasis on advent doctrine. The Seventh-day Adventists are the largest denomination that evolved from the Millerite movement.

The Seventh-day Adventist Church was begun in 1844 by a group of Adventists in Washington, New Hampshire, who observed the seventh-day Sabbath, that is, Saturday instead of Sunday, which is considered the first-day Sabbath. Initially, the Church was active only in the New England states. In 1855, Church headquarters moved to Battle Creek, Michigan, and, five years later, the name Seventh-day Adventists was formally adopted. In 1903, the Church headquarters moved to Washington, D.C.

Joseph Smith Home, Palmyra

CHAPTER 3

Joseph Smith and Mormonism

"He was purely a Yankee product and a great deal that was good in American folklore and thinking found its way into his writings and into his church. The cornerstone of his metaphysics was that virile concept which pervaded the whole American spirit and which was indeed the noblest ideal of Jesus and Buddha, that man is capable of eternal progress toward perfection.

But Joseph's conception of perfection was by no means exclusively spiritual. His kingdom of God was saturated with the Yankee enthusiasm for earthly blessings. No one more ingeniously than he combined Jewish and Christian mysticism with the goal of perpetual prosperity. 'Adam fell that men might be,' he wrote, 'and men are that they might have joy.' And for Joseph Smith joy came, not from melancholy contemplation, but from planning bigger and better cities, building bigger and nobler temples, and creating the nucleus of an American empire."[38]

Fawn M. Brodie, *No Man Knows My History*

75

Joseph Smith—Founder of Mormonism

Joseph Smith founded a religion that has withstood the test of time and is vigorous and growing in the twenty-first century. In *Joseph Smith, the First Mormon*, Donna Hill observes that:

> Joseph's church was only one of many, including the Seekers, Adventists, Scientists, and Campbellites, that were founded after the Revolution in response to the felt need for a religious reform. Like the church established by Joseph, some new movements attempted to restructure society in communal experiments, such as those conducted by the Fourierists, Swedenborgians, Cabet's Icarians, the Spiritualists, Robert Owen's New Harmony, and the Transcendentalists of Brook Farm, or in revisions of familial and sexual mores, such as those made by the Shakers, who renounced sexual intercourse; Josiah Warren's group, who combined free love and Spiritualism; and the followers of John Noyes, who practiced communal marriage.

> Such groups had the difficult task of establishing their unique organization within the larger society, and most eventually failed. Of all, Joseph developed the most extensive following. He had a message that filled a particular need and with it the ability to surround himself with vigorous, talented men and to inspire them to carry out his ideas.[39]

The Early Years

Joseph Smith was born in Sharon, Vermont, on December 23, 1805, the fourth child and third son of Joseph Smith, Sr., and Lucy Mack Smith. Smith, Sr., had difficulty earning a living farming the rocky soil of Vermont. He tried farming in several New England locations without success.

During the winter of 1812-13, young Joseph contracted typhoid fever and developed an abscess on his leg. The doctors decided to amputate the leg, but he was strong-willed even as a youth. He refused to let the doctors amputate, and he underwent an operation in which the diseased bone was removed without the benefit of anesthesia. The leg was saved, but he walked with a limp for the rest of his life. *Strong will*

In 1816, the family moved to Palmyra, New York, which became a boomtown on the Erie Canal. They were penniless upon their arrival in the small frontier village, but they were willing to work hard. Joseph, Sr., and his two oldest sons, Alvin and Hyrum, did odd jobs such as harvesting, well-digging, and making maple syrup.

Joseph Smith, Sr., and his wife Lucy, were religious people but did not belong to a particular denomination. The Protestant Church was undergoing considerable dissent in the early nineteenth century. Between 1814 and 1830, the Methodist Church divided into four parts. The Baptist Church split into even more groups.

Palmyra was in the middle of the Burned-over District, which experienced many religious revivals. Evangelists roamed the countryside. A Shaker community was thriving at Sodus Bay northeast of Palmyra, and Jemima Wilkinson, the Publick Universal Friend, had a successful community in the Keuka Lake area to the south.

Visitations

In 1820, young Joseph thought that he should join a church, but he could not find a denomination aligned with his understanding of the Gospel of Jesus Christ as set forth in the New Testament. Smith went into the woods by himself in response to the Epistle of James 1:5: "If any of you lack wisdom, let him ask God." He said that a pillar of light fell upon him:

Immediately I was seized by some power which entirely overcame me, and had such astonishing influence over me as to bind my tongue so that I could not speak. Thick darkness gathered around me, and it seemed to me for a time that I were doomed to sudden destruction ... just at this moment of great alarm, I saw a pillar of light exactly over my head, above the brightness of the sun, which gradually descended until it fell upon me.

It no sooner appeared than I found myself delivered from the enemy which held me bound. When the light rested upon me I saw two personages, whose brightness and glory defy all description, standing above me in the air. One of them spake unto me calling me by name and said—pointing to the other—"This is my beloved Son, hear him."

My object in going to inquire of the Lord was to know which of all the sects was right.... I was answered that I must join none of them, for they were all wrong, and the personage who addressed me said that all their creed were an abomination in His sight; that those professors were all corrupt, that "they draw near to me with their lips but their hearts are far from me; they teach for doctrines the commandments of men: having a form of godliness but they deny the power thereof."[40]

The location at which this visitation occurred became known as the Sacred Grove, a peaceful, wooded setting maintained today as a site for visitors. A second visitation occurred to Smith on September 21, 1823, in his room at home late on

78

The Sacred Grove, Palmyra

a Sunday evening:

> A personage appeared at my bedside, standing in the air, for his feet did not touch the floor. He had on a loose robe of most exquisite whiteness ... his whole person was glorious beyond description.... I was afraid; but the fear soon left me. He called me by name, and said that his name was Moroni; that God had work for me to do; and that my name should be had for good and evil among all nations, kindreds, and tongues....
>
> He said there was a book deposited, written upon gold plates, giving an account of the former inhabitants on this continent, and the sources from whence they sprang. He also said that the fullness of the everlasting Gospel was contained in it, as delivered by the Saviour to the ancient inhabitants; also that there were two stones in silver bows—and these stones, fastened to a breastplate, constituted what is called the Urim and Thummin—deposited with the plates; and the possession and use of these stones were what constituted "seers" in ancient and former times; and that God had prepared them for the purpose of translating the book.[41]

Smith went to the hill described in the vision, several miles south of Palmyra and east of the Palmyra-Canandaigua mail road. He found the plates and the breastplate with the Urim and Thummin under a large stone near the top of the hill on the west side. They were in a box made of stones cemented together. However, the messenger would not allow him to take the objects with him; he was not to have them for four more years. He was asked to meet the messenger at Hill Cumorah each year at the same time.

Joseph Smith Marries

In October 1825, Smith was hired to search for a silver mine in the Susquehanna Valley by Josiah Stowell of South Bainbridge, New York. Treasure hunting or "money-digging" was a fad at the time. He roomed with the Hale family in Harmony, Pennsylvania, near the perceived site of the mine. Smith became attracted to Emma Hale, a twenty-one-year-old schoolteacher. When the search for the mine was concluded, unsuccessfully, Smith worked for Stowell at South Bainbridge. He frequently visited Emma at Harmony. Smith and Emma were married on January 18, 1827; they moved in with his parents in Palmyra.

Translation and Dissemination of the Messages on the Plates

On September 21, 1827, Smith went to Hill Cumorah, where the messenger Moroni gave him the plates, the Urim and Thummin, and the breastplate. He began the laborious task of translating the plates with one of the "seer" stones. Smith entrusted a loyal neighbor, Martin Harris, to take the transcript of the translation to New York City for evaluation; Charles Anthon of Columbia College said they were "Egyptian, Chaldaic, Assyric, and Arabic."[42]

In 1829, Smith chose Egbert B. Grandin of Palmyra, publisher of the Wayne *Sentinel*, to publish the Book of Mormon. Martin Harris mortgaged his farm for $3,000 to pay Grandin for 5,000 leather-bound copies of the 590-page book. As described in the introduction to the Book of Mormon:

> The Book of Mormon is a volume of holy scripture comparable to the Bible. It is a record of God's dealings with the ancient inhabitants of the Americas and contains, as does the

Martin Harris Homestead, Palmyra

Bible, the fullness of the everlasting Gospel.

The book was written by many ancient
prophets by the spirit of prophecy and revelation. Their words, written on gold plates, were
quoted and abridged by a prophet-historian
named Mormon. The record gives an account
of two great civilizations. One came from
Jerusalem in 600 BC, and afterward separated
into two nations, known as the Nephites and
the Lamanites. The other came much earlier
when the Lord confounded the tongues at the
Tower of Babel. This group is known as the
Jaredites. After thousands of years, all were
destroyed except the Lamanites, and they were
the primary ancestors of the American Indians.

The crowning event recorded in the Book of
Mormon is the personal ministry of the Lord
Jesus Christ among the Nephites soon after
His resurrection. It puts forth the doctrines of
the Gospel, outlines of the plan of salvation,
and tells men what they must do to gain peace
in this life and eternal salvation in the life to
come.[43]

Two testimonies were prepared to document the beginnings of Mormonism. The first one, "The Testimony of Three
Witnesses" was signed by three of Smith's early followers:
Oliver Cowdery, David Whitmer, and Martin Harris. On April
6, 1830, at the organization of the Church of Jesus Christ of
Latter-day Saints at the Whitmer Farm in Fayette, a second
testimony was prepared and formally signed by eight witnesses:

Be it known to all nations, kindreds, tongues,
and people, unto whom this work shall come:

That Joseph Smith, Jun., the translator of this work has shown unto us the plates of which hath been spoken, which have the appearance of gold; and as many of the leaves as the said Smith has translated we did handle with our hands; and we also saw the engravings thereon, all of which has the appearance of ancient work, and of the curious workmanship.

And this we bear record with words of soberness, that the said Smith has shown unto us, for we have seen and hefted, and know of a surety that the said Smith has got the plates of which we have spoken. And we give our names to the world, to witness unto the world, that which we have seen. And we lie not, God bearing witness of it.[44]

Christian Whitmer	Jacob Whitmer	Peter Whitmer, Jun.
John Whitmer	Hyrum Smith	Joseph Smith, Sen.
Samuel H. Smith	Hiram Page	

Now known as the Church of Jesus Christ of Latter-day Saints, members are called "Mormons" because the messenger Moroni's father, Mormon, was the major compiler of the ancient records.

The Church Moves to the Midwest

Joseph Smith and his followers were the target of sneers and harassment. Many of the residents of the area around Palmyra questioned the new religion. Mormons were resented for their self-righteousness and their thoughts of superior destiny. Smith considered moving from Palmyra. A successful settlement had been established at Kirtland, Ohio, just east of

Whitmer Homestead, Fayette

Cleveland. Sidney Rigdon, one of the leaders of the western outpost, became a Mormon.

On January 2, 1831, Smith had a revelation to move the Church, which consisted of sixty members, from Palmyra to Kirtland. The Church in Kirtland, which had been founded by missionaries, had grown to 100 members. The first Mormon Temple was built in Kirtland, and Smith established a Mormon bank there.

Resistance to the Mormon Church also existed in Ohio, and on March 24, 1832, Smith was dragged from his home and tarred and feathered. Sidney Rigdon was beaten severely. Smith encountered many differences of opinion among his followers and numerous challenges to his authority. The level of tension was higher in Kirtland than in Palmyra.

Smith sent a missionary, Parley Pratt, to Jackson County, Missouri, to evaluate a site for Zion where they would settle. Missouri had been a state for ten years but was still open frontier country. The Mormons moving into the region were harassed by the residents, who swore at them, vandalized their property, and fired shots into their houses. Mormon homes were pulled down, and Mormon men were whipped, hit with rifle butts, and tarred and feathered. Mormons were not welcome in Missouri either. They looked for another location in which to settle.

In May 1839, many of the Kirtland members of the Church moved to Commerce, Illinois, which they renamed Nauvoo. Mormons built their second temple in Nauvoo. The City of Nauvoo received a charter from the State of Illinois that gave it considerable autonomy. Between 1841 and 1844, Nauvoo grew so rapidly that it became the largest city in Illinois, even larger than Chicago.

Smith controlled all land sales to members of his church. He had to balance following the word of the Lord with making money to keep the enterprise going. Brigham Young was placed in charge of the missionary effort of sending members of the Church abroad to spread the word of the Church. Of

Smith's apostles, Young had the most business acumen. Eventually, he was given the responsibility for managing the Church's financial operations.

The practice of plural marriage, polygamy, was inaugurated by the church in 1842, a practice that caused considerable dissension within the Church and resentment outside of it.

Death of the Founder

On June 7, 1844, the Nauvoo *Expositor* published its first issue openly criticizing Smith's leadership of the Church. Smith and the city council authorized the destruction of the Nauvoo *Expositor's* press. Smith and his brother, Hyrum, were jailed in Carthage, Illinois, for the suppression of the Nauvoo *Expositor*. On June 27, 1844, a mob stormed the jail in the courthouse. The guards, who were in collusion with the attackers, fired into the mob at a distance of twenty feet without hitting anyone. The mob climbed the stairs to the Smith brothers' cell.

Smith, Lieutenant-General of the Nauvoo Legion, got out his six-shooter, and Hyrum sprang for his pistol. Hyrum was killed by a shot through the closed door to their cell. Smith opened the door and emptied his pistol into the crowd in the passageway. He then went to the window, where he was shot both from inside the cell and from outside the courthouse and fatally wounded.

The Move to Utah

In 1845, the Council of Twelve announced that the Church would leave Illinois. On December 27, 1847, Brigham Young was installed as president of the Church of Jesus Christ of Latter-day Saints to carry on the work of Joseph Smith. Young decided to lead his people to a location "so unpromising that nobody will covet it." In July 1847, the Great Salt Lake Basin was chosen as the home of the Mormons.

Young led an advance party of 143 men and three women

in seventy-two Conestoga wagons to their new Zion. The Great Salt Lake had no outlet to the sea, and the surrounding area was no Eden. Nevertheless, as he and his advance party approached the area, Young announced, "This is the place." In 1847, the region was under the jurisdiction of Mexico. It was called the Utah Territory when it became part of the United States at the signing of the Treaty of Guadalupe Hidalgo one year later.

Moving the Mormons across the country and building 450 houses for a population of 5,000 in one year contributed to Brigham Young's reputation as one of the foremost colonists in history. The Mormons planted 5,000 acres of grain that were attacked by crickets. Nothing that they did defeated the scourge of crickets. They resorted to prayer. A large flock of sea gulls descended from the western sky to consume the crickets. The Mormons were saved. To this day, the sea gull is one of the symbols of the Mormon Church. Another symbol is the beehive, exemplifying the industry of all members of a community working together for the common good. Brigham Young's home was called Beehive House.

During the first ten years in the West, Mormons built 135 communities with a population of 76,335, not only in Utah, but also in California, Idaho, New Mexico, and Wyoming. Between 1856 and 1880, 4,075 converts came from Europe, principally from England and Scandinavia. Young built the Mormon Tabernacle, the Salt Lake City temple that took forty years to complete, as well as a fine theatre. Choruses, orchestras, and debating societies were established. He sponsored a railroad, a telegraph company, and factories. Mormons organized the "State" of Deseret and asked to be admitted to the Union in 1849. Instead, the Territory of Utah was established in 1850. Brigham Young was appointed governor by President Millard Fillmore.

Difficulties with the Federal Government and the Death of Brigham Young

In response to rumors that Utah Territory planned to secede from the Union, U.S. Army General Albert Sidney Johnston was sent to depose Young as Governor of Utah Territory in 1857. Young gave up the title of Governor but retained effective control of the Territory through the Mormon Church. In 1861, Johnston's troops were recalled to fight the Civil War, and Johnston became one of the Confederacy's leading Generals. In 1862, an act of Congress outlawed polygamy, but the Mormon Church refused to comply with the law. Friction with the federal government continued for years.

Brigham Young died on August 29, 1877, at the age of seventy-six, after directing the spiritual and secular affairs of the Church for thirty-three years. He attracted thousands of converts to Utah and led the region's agricultural and industrial advances. He founded cities, established universities, and sponsored art, music, and literature in the Great Salt Lake basin. He authorized experiments in agriculture and in irrigation, which was critically needed in the region. Young, a polygamist, had fifty-six children. His epitaph reads: "Brigham Young ... Prophet ... Statesman ... Pioneer."

Difficulties Resolved

In 1887, Mormon voters were disenfranchised, and all property of the Mormon Church was seized by the federal government. The next generation of the Twelve Apostles of the Church wanted peace and statehood, so they capitulated in 1890 as ordered by the U.S. Supreme Court. They retained their concept of celestial marriage solemnized in a temple that makes a family relationship an association for eternity but gave up the practice of polygamy. In 1896, voting rights and Church property were restored, and statehood was granted that year.

Of the religions founded in the United States, the Mormon Church has grown and prospered like no other. In *No Man*

Knows My History, Fawn M. Brodie discusses the reason for this success:

> But this legend is not enough to explain the vigor and tenacity of the Mormon Church. Before his death, Joseph had established an evangelical socialism, in which every man worked feverously to build the Kingdom of God upon earth. This has grown into a vast pyramidal organization, in which the workers finance the church, advertise it, and do everything but govern it.
>
> The Mormons are still bent on building the Kingdom of God, and everyone from the twelve-year-old deacon to the eighty-year-old high priest is made to feel that upon him depends the realization of the ideal. Here as in no other church in America, the people are the church and the church the people. It is not only work and sacrifice, but a sense of participation and responsibility that generates the steadfast Mormon loyalty.[45]

The early history of the Mormons was characterized by misunderstandings by the populace of the regions in which they settled. They were driven out of Ohio and Missouri by violence. After enduring further persecution in Illinois, they trekked to the West. Over the course of their history, Mormons have been harassed by state militia in two states, have been the target of a U.S. Army expedition, and have had their property confiscated. For over forty years, they were persecuted for their practice of polygamy. Throughout it all, they have endured. In fact, their difficulties may have made them stronger.

Life-sized statues of Joseph and Hyrum Smith stand on

Temple Square in Salt Lake City. A commemorative tablet at the base of Joseph's statue contains an excerpt from his teachings:

> The glory of God is intelligence.
> This is the work and the glory of God; to bring to pass the immortality and eternal life of man.
> Adam fell that man might be; and men are that they might have joy.
> The intelligence of spirits had no beginning, neither will it have an end.

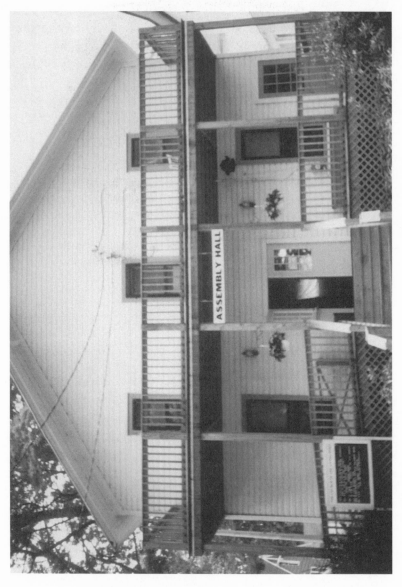

Assembly Hall, Lily Dale

CHAPTER 4

The Fox Sisters and Spiritualism

"Upper New York State was the region chosen by the spirits for their revelations because the people who lived there were willing to receive them and to accept their messages. Initiates in such matters were therefore not surprised in 1848 when a small frame house in Hydesville, near Rochester, became the scene of some strange occurrences.

The chosen instruments of the spirits were humble folk—a Methodist farmer, John Fox, and his wife, and their two little girls, Margaret, aged thirteen, and Katherine, aged twelve. When Fox moved his family into the house in December 1847, the dwelling was already haunted, or so it was said...."[46]

Earl Wesley Fornell, *The Unhappy Medium*

The Fox Sisters—Spiritualism

Many mark the beginnings of Spiritualism in the United States with the activities of two young girls in Hydesville, New York, in 1848. In *Charmers and Cranks*, Ishbel Ross comments on these beginnings:

> When Margaret and Kate Fox of Rochester became famous in the late 1840s for their mysterious rappings, they helped to establish Spiritualism as a serious cult in the United States, and their curious manifestations baffled some of the shrewdest men of their day. John Fox, their father, was a hard-headed Methodist who found it difficult to accept the strange occurrences under his own roof as his daughters became the elite of the spirit world. It all began when he took a small farmhouse that was said to be haunted. Years earlier, a peddler was supposed to have been murdered on the premises, and now neighbors believed that his ghost walked the night....[47]

John Fox, his wife, Margaret, and their two youngest daughters, Margaretta and Katherine, moved to Rochester from Bath, Ontario, in 1844. In December 1847, the blacksmith and his family moved into a house on the corner of Parker and Hydesville Roads in the hamlet of Hydesville, near Newark.

Michael Weekman, who had lived in the house in 1846 and 1847, moved out because his family had heard mysterious noises, and he had failed to find the source of the rapping sounds. Shortly after blowing out the candle in her bedroom one night, Weekman's eight-year-old daughter had felt cold, clammy hands on her face. The neighbors thought that the house was haunted. John Fox and his wife were devout Methodists; they did not believe the rumors.

Beginnings of Spiritualism

In early 1848, the Fox family heard mysterious rappings in the walls of their house for the first time. Margaretta and Kate both felt cold hands pass over their faces. On March 31, 1848, the two teenage girls, one fourteen and one thirteen, decided that they would attempt to communicate with the source of the rappings. Kate called out, "Here Mr. Splitfoot, do as I do," and snapped her finger three times. Three raps were heard in response. Margaretta clapped her hands four times and said, "Do just as I do." Four raps were heard on the wall near her. Then Kate held up four fingers and asked, "How many fingers am I holding out?" They heard four raps. Kate pointed out to her mother that the source of the knocking could see as well as hear.

They received no response to the question, "Are you a man?" However, they received a multiple-rap response to the question, "Are you a spirit?" William Duesler, a neighbor who devised a code by assigning numbers to letters of the alphabet, learned that the spirit's name was Charles B. Rosma. He also learned that he was a peddler who had been murdered in the house and buried in the cellar. When Duesler and several other neighbors dug in the cellar the next morning, they found a human skull, human hair, and quicklime.

Some people believed that modern Spiritualism was born that evening of March 31, 1848. They believed that the "conversation" that night with the spirit of Charles Rosma was the first communication between this world and the next. Sir Arthur Conan Doyle referred to the event as "one of the great points of psychic evolution." That spring, the rappings became more frequent, and people began to visit the house. One day there were 500 visitors.

In *The Spirit Rappers*, Herbert G. Jackson, Jr., observes:

> In July of 1848, two events of note took place
> less than twenty-five miles apart in western
> New York. Elizabeth Cady Stanton and

Lucretia Mott convened the first women's rights convention at Seneca Falls, and the cellar floor of the empty Hydesville "spook house" was ripped up in a two-day quest for the corporeal remains of a murdered peddler.

The period was one of religious and social ferment, a period that had witnessed the rise—and in some cases the fall—of Mormonism, mesmerism, Shakerism, Fourierism, phrenology, Swedenborgianism. Thousands of Millerites had believed that 1843 or 1844 would see the end of the world.

It was also a time of serious economic depression and recovery, abolitionism, feminism, and temperance crusades....[48]

Capitalizing on the Rappings

The girls' older sister, Leah Fox Fish, decided to capitalize on the attention that her family was receiving in the press. Leah, a widow who lived in Rochester, scheduled "sittings" to display her sisters' talents. People began to call these sittings "séances." Leah moved her young sisters into her home. In November 1849, she rented Corinthian Hall, the largest hall in Rochester, for public demonstrations of her sisters' ability to communicate with the next world.

Advertising circulars for the meeting promised a "full explanation of the nature and history of the mysterious noises supposed to be supernatural, which have caused so much excitement in this city ... The 'mysterious agencies' have promised to give the public an actual demonstration of the sounds, so that they may know that the sounds are neither made nor controlled by human beings."[49]

Two of Leah's friends were among the earliest to spread the word of Spiritualism. Isaac Post and his wife, who were

Quakers, were the first invited to hear the rappings.
E. W. Capron, a young businessman from Auburn, was another of the early believers.

Many people had difficulty believing the Fox sisters' revelations. Skeptics attempted to disprove them, including three doctors from Buffalo. The Buffalo *Commercial Advertiser* published a letter prepared by three physicians from the University of Buffalo. They concluded that:

> Now, it was sufficiently clear that the rappings were not vocal sounds; these could not have been produced without movements of the respiratory muscles, which would at once lead to detection. Hence, excluding vocal sounds, the only possible source of the noises in question, produced, as we have seen they must be, by voluntary muscular contractions, is in one of the more movable articulations of the skeleton. From the anatomical construction of the voluntary muscles, this explanation remains the only alternative.

> By an analysis, prosecuted in this manner, we arrive at the conviction that the rappings, assuming they are not spiritual, are produced by the action of the will, through voluntary movements of the joints.

> Various facts may be cited to show that the motion of the joints, under certain circumstances, is adequate to produce the phenomena of the rappings; but we need not now refer to these. By a curious coincidence, after arriving at the above conclusion respecting the source of the sounds, an instance has fallen under our observation, which demonstrates the fact that

noises precisely identical with the spiritual rappings may be produced by the knee joints.[50]

The doctors cited the example of a woman from Buffalo who could make rapping sounds with her knees. Leah Fox Fish responded by suggesting that the doctors examine Margaretta during a séance. They learned that there were no raps if Margaretta's feet, while she was seated, were placed on chairs in front of her, and her knees were held firmly. Leah explained that the spirits didn't respond because they thought that Margaretta was being mistreated. Margaretta became nervous and tired from the negative comments in the press and from the publicity that the doctors had received.

Leah took the girls on a tour of Albany, Troy, and New York City. In Albany, a minister accused the Fox sisters of blasphemy against the Holy Scriptures. He filed a complaint against them with the police, who took no action. However, an unruly mob disrupted their séance. Margaretta's and Kate's demonstrations in New York were attended by James Fenimore Cooper, William Cullen Bryant, and New York *Tribune* editor Horace Greeley.

The interest of Greeley and his wife, Mary, in the Fox sisters was triggered by their grief over the death of a son and their hope of communicating with him. The Greeleys invited the Fox sisters to hold séances in their home. Their guests included Jenny Lind, the Swedish nightingale. Mary Greeley sincerely believed that she had been able to communicate with her son. Horace Greeley didn't actually believe that contact had been made, but his name associated with the cause of Spiritualism helped to promote the Fox sisters. Greeley documented his thoughts about the sisters:

Their conduct and bearing is as unlike that of deceivers as possible, and we think that no one acquainted with them could believe them at all capable of engaging in so daring, impious, and shameful a juggle as this would be if they had caused the sounds. And it is not possible that such a juggle should have been so long perpetrated in public, and yet escape detection. A juggler performs one feat quickly and hurries to another. He does not devote week after week to doing the same thing over and over deliberately, in view of hundreds who sit beside him or confronting him in broad daylight, not to enjoy but to detect his trick.

A deceiver naturally avoids conversation on the subject of his knavery, but these ladies converse freely and fully with regard to the origin of these "rappings" in their dwelling years ago, the various sensations they caused, the neighborhood excitement created, the progress of the developments—what they have seen, heard, and experienced first to last.

If all were false, they could not fail to have involved themselves in a labyrinth of blasting contradictions, as each separately gives accounts of the most astounding occurrences at this or that time. Persons foolish enough to commit themselves without reserve or caution could not have deferred a thought of thorough self-exposure for a single week....[51]

Greeley offered to finance Kate's education. She went to school, but she tired of it and returned to her Spiritualist activities.

Margaretta Falls in Love and Marries

In the fall of 1852, Margaretta Fox and her mother traveled to Philadelphia, where she met Arctic explorer Elisha Kent Kane. Kane, member of a leading Philadelphia family, had sailed as ship's doctor on an 1850 expedition to find the lost English explorer, Sir John Franklin. They failed to find Franklin, but the expedition placed Kane's name before the American public. He was in line to command the next search expedition to the Arctic.

Kane visited Margaretta and her mother at their hotel and was immediately captivated by the young Spiritualist. For him, it was love at first sight. He pursued her, encouraging her to go to school and to give up her interest in Spiritualism. During the early spring of 1853, Margaretta realized that she was in love with Kane and decided to do as he had suggested, to return to school and to give up her Spiritualist activities. Kane promised to marry her upon his return from his next voyage to the Arctic. In May 1853, he sailed for the North.

In Kane's absence, Margaretta went to school in Philadelphia and later in Albany. Kane's expedition was unsuccessful in finding Franklin; however, they discovered Kennedy Channel, which Robert E. Peary used on a later expedition. Kane's trip concluded with a 1,300 mile, eighty-three-day trek to a Danish town in Greenland.

Upon his return to New York, Kane made no attempt to contact Margaretta. His family did not agree with his courting her. His parents looked upon her as their son's friend, not his fiancée. Margaretta was shocked by this treatment. However, Kane prevailed, and he and Margaretta were married in a Quaker ceremony. Shortly after their marriage, Kane sailed for England to report to Lady Franklin about the search for her husband and to visit several scientific societies. He became ill and stayed in England only a short time. Upon his return, he went to Havana to recuperate in the sun.

On February 16, 1857, Kane died. Upon her husband's death at the age of thirty-six, Margaretta gave up her

Spiritualist demonstrations. In accordance with her husband's wishes, she became a Catholic. Kane suggested this because he thought that it would end her connection with Spiritualism, and, briefly, it did. Subsequently, she went on a tour to England with Kate and, while there, demonstrated her psychic powers to Thomas Carlyle.

Rejecting Spiritualism and Then Recanting

Upon their return home from England, Kate and Margaretta renounced the methods by which they had inspired the Spiritualist movement. On October 21, 1888, at the Academy of Music in New York, Margaret gave a demonstration of how she and her sister had made the rapping sounds. She removed the shoe and stocking from her right leg and showed the audience how she made the noises with her big toe. She said that her sister, Leah, had urged her two younger sisters not to reveal the secret. The New York *Herald* commented on the event:

> By throwing life and enthusiasm into her big toe, Mrs. Margaret Fox Kane produced loud spirit rappings ... and dealt a blow to Spiritualism, that huge and worldwide fraud which she and her sister Kate founded in 1848. Both sisters were present, and both denounced Spiritualism as a monstrous imposition and cheat. The great building was crowded, and the wildest excitement prevailed at times. Hundreds of Spiritualists had come to see the originators of their faith destroy it at one stroke. They were greatly agitated at times and hissed freely....

> Mrs. Kane's confession: That I have been instrumental in perpetuating the fraud of Spiritualism upon a too confiding public, many of you already know. It is the greatest

sorrow of my life. It is a late day now, but I am
prepared to tell the truth, and nothing but the
truth, so help me God....

Many here will scorn me; but if they knew
the sorrow of my past life they would pity,
not condemn. When I began this deception, I
was too young to know right from wrong. I
hope God Almighty will forgive me and those
silly enough to believe in Spiritualism.[52]

On November 20, 1889, Margaretta recanted and said that
she really did have psychic powers, but that she had been
talked into saying that she and her sister made the rapping
sounds with their big toes. Margaretta said that she had lied
when she spoke out against Spiritualism:

Would to God that I could undo the injustice
that I did the cause of Spiritualism. I was
under the strong mental influence of persons
who hated it. They made me say things that
were untrue.... At the time I spoke against
Spiritualism, I was in great need of money.
Persons I prefer not to name took advantage of
this. The excitement also helped upset my
mind.... It was all false. My belief in
Spiritualism has not changed. When I said
those dreadful things, I was not responsible for
my words.[53]

They were welcomed back into the Spiritualism movement and remained active in it until their death.

Growth of Spiritualism
Many factors contributed to the growth of Spiritualism in the
United States, particularly in the Northeast and Midwest.

During the 1840s and 1850s, many economic, political, and social changes happened in America. Financial panics occurred in 1837 and 1857. A new generation of political leaders was taking office, replacing the generation that had led the country in its early years. Population and urbanization were increasing rapidly, particularly with the growth in immigration in the 1840s.

In *Spiritualism in Antebellum America*, Bret E. Carroll summarized the impact of these changes:

> These unsettling developments combined to produce spiritual malaise, discomfort, discontent, and above all a search for order among many Americans. Most of those attracted to Spiritualism found their deities distant, their cultural and social surroundings disturbing, and their ministers and churches ineffectual in addressing the resulting uneasiness.
>
> Fearing that spiritual values and religious institutions were losing their influence on American society, they experimented with new religious ideas and practices and joined their contemporaries in a variety of cultural, social, moral, and scientific (or quasi-scientific) reform movements. They hoped to find more satisfying forms of religious belief and expression and, like many religious Americans before and after them, to resacralize a society and a cosmos that they feared was spiritually empty.
>
> This restless searching ... was a major theme of nineteenth-century culture. Those who embraced the Spiritualist religion often had backgrounds suggesting restless disapproval

of the status quo and an openness to new and progressive philosophies. They usually came from such liberal religions as Swedenborgianism, Universalism, Quakerism, and, to a lesser extent, Unitarianism, Transcendentalism, and Rationalism, each of which contributed not only members to the Spiritualist movement but also ideas to its religious ideology.

They often moved through one or more of these beliefs before drifting to Spiritualism. They also tended to be committed to one or more of such causes as temperance, women's rights, abolitionism, communitarianism, phrenology, and mesmerism, as well as dietary, dress, marriage, and medical reform. Their desire for order and spiritual fulfillment eventually led them to seek communion with spirits and to create their own religion.[54]

Commercialization and industrialization began to change the nation dramatically beginning in the 1830s. The growth of technology displayed by the building of manufacturing plants, railroads, and telegraph systems required the public at large to adapt. The expansion of a capitalistic market economy led to an increase in materialism and economic uncertainty. Moral values seemed to be declining.

In *Spiritualism and Society*, Geoffrey K. Nelson comments on the phenomena of Spiritualism:

During the period of most rapid expansion [1848-1870] there was no central organization of Spiritualists, and there were very few local organizations of any permanence. The movement in this period was virile and fluid in the extreme, consisting of local groups of enthusiasts who seldom formalized their organization into anything like a church. Beyond a vague belief in the existence of God, the immortality of the human spirit, and the ability of spirits to communicate with the living, there was little agreement on doctrine.

The spirits themselves had various opinions regarding the nature of God and varied answers to other theological and natural problems. This was not strange to Spiritualists though since they believed that the human soul does not become all wise on entering the spirit world, but takes with it all its earthly preconceptions and beliefs. Only gradually do spirits acquire further knowledge. It is therefore not strange to find that in their beliefs about God, the Spiritualists varied from the agnostic position through Unitarianism to conventional Christian beliefs.[55]

According to the estimates of N. P. Willis, editor of the *Home Journal*, in 1853, 40,000 Spiritualists were active in New York in approximately 300 circles. He estimated that in Brooklyn and Williamsburg twice that number of circles existed.

Decline of Spiritualism
The decline of Spiritualism had many facets. Examples of mediums who used fraud and deception became public knowledge, disillusioning many followers, particularly intellectual supporters. Many churches had attacked the Spiritualist movement from the beginning, implying that it was the work of the devil, or, in any case, not really Christian.

The press, with its tendency for sensationalism, was particularly unkind to the movement. Newspapers tended to neglect the Spiritualist interpretation of an event and instead concentrated on their own viewpoint on the phenomena of the movement. Spiritualism was not permitted to be demonstrated in public in the State of Alabama. Generally, Spiritualism was not perceived to have lived up to its early promise.

In *The Heyday of Spiritualism*, Slater Brown provides an overview of the decline of Spiritualism:

> Though America had produced the first and some of the most remarkable mediums, the lack of any competent and disinterested body of investigators left the Spiritualists without any critical ballast to keep their ship on an even keel. As their numbers increased (by 1855, Spiritualists claimed over two million adherents to the faith), so did their critical standards decline.

> Mediums gifted with genuine clairvoyant powers became lax, now that there was no real pressure to use them. Like ... clairvoyants, they drew on their own imaginations during a séance rather than on their psychic faculties. Daydreams ... were frequently offered as as inspired visions of life.... Physical manifestations, inexplicable as many of them were, came to be ignored as of secondary importance to the communications from exalted spirits of the past.

> Spiritualist journals (by 1856, there were scores) published any report of psychic experience that drifted into the office, with no effort on the part of the editors to check the information or credibility of the correspon-

dent. Occasionally, hoaxes, perpetrated by some prankster, would occupy a journal's pages.... With so many diverse and corrupting elements at work—commercialism, over-credulity, secondhand evidence, hoaxes, and downright fraud—it was difficult to separate the chaff from the wheat, the false from the genuine.[56]

The Later Years

In their later years, the Fox sisters had no regular source of income. Kate and Margaretta attempted to earn money as mediums, but their income from this activity was small. Both sisters drank heavily. Kate died on July 2, 1892, in a seedy rooming house in New York. Margaretta, who was ill and living in poverty, died on March 8, 1893, at the home of a friend in Brooklyn. They were buried in Greenwood Cemetery. The women, who were celebrities in their youth, died in obscurity.

On November 21, 1904, a group of children playing in the cellar of the Fox home in Hydesville found an over fifty-year-old skeleton when a foundation wall crumbled. Many area residents believed that this was the skeleton of the peddler murdered in the house in 1848. People wanted to believe the stories that had circulated for over half a century.

In 1915, the Hydesville house was moved to the Spiritualist camp at Lily Dale in the Chautauqua region where it was destroyed by a fire in 1955. A marker on the site at Lily Dale notes "The Birthplace of Modern Spiritualism—Upon This Site Stood the Hydesville Cottage, the Home of the Fox Sisters." It includes the words, "There is no death; there are no dead."

Jemima Wilkinson House, Town of Jerusalem

CHAPTER 5

Jemima Wilkinson and the Universal Friends

"Jemima Wilkinson was one of three notable religious innovators who appeared in New England in the opening years of the American Revolution. The other two—John Murray, founder of Universalism in America, and Mother Ann Lee of the Shakers—left more enduring marks in American religious history, but Jemima Wilkinson, the only native American of the trio, also merits serious attention. This self-educated, penniless woman, who called herself the Publick Universal Friend, became a successful, nondenominational, evangelical preacher.

Supported by people of wealth and social position whom she induced to follow her, she was the first American-born woman to found a religious society. Leading her group into the wilderness of western New York, she pioneered in settling that region as well as in attempting to establish a religious community apart from the secular world. Born just after the middle of the eighteenth century and living almost through the second decade of the nineteenth, Jemima Wilkinson deserves to be ranked with the small group of outstanding women of the colonial period."[57]

Herbert A. Wisbey, Jr., *Pioneer Prophetess*

Jemima Wilkinson—The Publick Universal Friend

Jemima Wilkinson, the first American-born woman to found a religious sect, led a religious community whose members were pioneers in opening central and western New York. In *Pioneer Prophetess*, Herbert A. Wisbey, Jr., makes the following observations about Wilkinson:

> Contrary to the impressions created by legends and folklore, Jemima Wilkinson undoubtedly was sincere in her belief that her call to preach was divinely inspired. Although she was handicapped by an inadequate education and a limited breadth of experience, her religious fanaticism, combined with such natural attributes as a dynamic personality, a sense of the dramatic, and effective speaking ability, made her a highly successful evangelical preacher.
>
> To the chagrin of some men, she demonstrated that a woman could stand before large crowds and preach a sermon that many found moving. She was accepted as a leader of both men and women and inspired one of the earliest settlements in western New York. Few women of the colonial period of American history have matched the accomplishments of Jemima Wilkinson, the Publick Universal Friend.[58]

The Early Years

Jemima, the eighth of twelve children of Jeremiah and Amey Whipple Wilkinson, was born in Cumberland, Rhode Island, on November 29, 1752. She was named for one of Job's daughters and was raised as a Quaker. Amey Wilkinson died giving birth to her twelfth child when Jemima was twelve years old. It was a time of stress for the motherless family. Jemima's sister Patience was disowned by the Quakers for

110

giving birth out of wedlock, and her brothers Stephen and Jeptha were disowned for having "frequented trainings for military service and endeavored to justify the same."

When Wilkinson was seventeen, George Whitefield, who initiated the first Great Awakening in the colonies, spoke in Providence, Rhode Island, and Attleboro, Massachusetts. It is not certain that she heard him speak in nearby Attleboro; nevertheless, she was influenced by him. In her early twenties, Wilkinson was further influenced by the New Light Baptists, who emphasized individual inspiration and enlightenment through the Holy Spirit.

In February 1776, Wilkinson was issued a warning to mend her ways by the Society of Friends for not attending Friends' meetings and for not speaking the Quaker language, using "thee" and "thou." In August 1776, she was disowned by the Smithfield Meeting of the Quakers and began an intensive meditation and study of the Bible, to the exclusion of all social contacts.

Wilkinson became ill, and it wasn't clear whether her illness was due to severe emotional stress or if it were a condition caused by typhus. Dr. Man from Attleboro verified that she had a fever and was seriously ill. His observations were documented:

> Her case was like one other he knew of that the fever being translated to the head. She rose with different ideas than what she had when the fever was general, and she conceived the idea that she had been dead and was raised up for extraordinary purposes, and got well fast— but that she had been dead. None of her friends or attendants had any apprehension or thought of her having been dead, but she was for some time after considered by her friends not to be in her right mind.[59]

Wilkinson recorded the experience of her illness in her papers:

> The heavens were opened and she saw two archangels descending from the East, with golden crowns upon their heads, clothed in long white robes down to the feet; bringing a sealed pardon from the living God; and putting trumpets to their mouths, proclaimed saying room, room, room, in the many mansions of eternal glory for thee and everyone....
>
> And the angels said, the time is at hand when God will lift up his hand a second time, to recover the remnant of his people whose day is not yet over; and the angels said the spirit of life from God had descended to Earth to warn a lost and guilty, perishing dying world to flee from the wrath which is to come; and to give an invitation to the lost sheep of the house of Israel to come home; and was waiting to assume the body which God has prepared, for the spirit to dwell in....
>
> And then taking her leave of the family between the hours of nine and ten in the morning dropped the dying flesh and yielded up the Ghost. And according to the declaration of the angels—the Spirit took full possession of the body it now animates.[60]

In Jemima's opinion, she had died and come back to life; furthermore, some biographers claim that she thought she hadn't just come back to life, but that she had returned as the Second Coming of Christ. She no longer considered herself Jemima Wilkinson; she called herself the Publick Universal Friend or just the Universal Friend.

Early Preaching Experiences

Wilkinson preached in Rhode Island and nearby Massachusetts and soon branched out to Connecticut. By 1781, she was preaching in Philadelphia, where her followers included both well-to-do and common people. Her appearance was described in the March 1787 New Haven *Gazette and* Connecticut *Magazine*:

> She is about the middle size of woman, not genteel in her person, rather awkward in her carriage; her complexion good, her eyes remarkably black and brilliant, her hair black and waving with beautiful ringlets upon her neck and shoulders; her features are regular, and the whole of her face thought by many to be perfectly beautiful.

> As she is not supposed to be of either sex, so this neutrality is manifest in her personal appearance. She wears no cap, letting her hair hang down as has been described. She wears her neckcloth like a man; her chemise is buttoned around the neck and wrists. Her outside garment is a robe, under which it is said she wears an expensive dress, the fashion of which is made to correspond neither with that of a man or woman....[61]

Another individual who heard her preach described her as "straight, well made, with light complexion, black eyes, round face, and chestnut dark hair." She wasn't a refined or erudite person, but she was confident and sincere. One of her strengths was an incredible memory, which permitted her to recite lengthy sections of the Bible.

In Wilkinson's early days as a preacher, she attempted, without success, faith healing. On at least one occasion, in

May 1780, she attempted to raise a person from the dead. Susannah Potter, daughter of Judge William Potter, died while still a young woman. Wilkinson asked for the lid of the coffin to be raised while she knelt by the coffin in prayer. She was not successful in her efforts. She blamed the failure on the insufficient faith of her followers. This was the last recorded attempt by Wilkinson to raise a person from the dead.

Nevertheless, Judge William Potter, town clerk of South Kingston, Rhode Island, and Chief Justice of the Court of Common Pleas for King's County, became an early Wilkinson supporter. Another supporter from South Kingston was Captain James Parker, a landowner and Justice of the Peace. Two of her lieutenants were from Connecticut, Ruth Pritchard of Wallingford and Sarah Richards of Watertown, known as Sarah Friend, who became a preacher and second in command to the Universal Friend.

The Move to the Finger Lakes Region

Wilkinson decided to move her religious followers away from populated areas and recommended that they "shun the company and conversation of the wicked world." She wrote to James Parker asking for suggestions; she was considering a "wilderness" location. The sect heard glowing reports of the Finger Lakes Region from members of General Sullivan's expedition of 1779.

In 1785, Wilkinson's brother, Jeptha Wilkinson, explored the region, and another Universal Friend traced General Sullivan's route the following year. Upon his return, Jemima and her principal members decided to locate in Genesee country, and James Parker was selected to lead a group to pick a site.

An advance party of twenty-five, led by Parker, established a settlement in 1788 on the Keuka Lake outlet into Seneca Lake, just west of the present village of Dresden. Parker's party was attracted by a waterfall, which they used to power a gristmill and a sawmill, the first mills in the region.

The Publick Universal Friend left Worcester, Massachusetts, to join the settlement in 1789, but encountered flood-swollen Bushkill Creek, fifty miles west of Worcester, and almost drowned when her carriage filled with water. She returned to Worcester and made the trip successfully in the spring of 1790.

The Friends' settlement, a tract of 14,000 acres that they called City Hill, was centered on a knoll about a mile south of the Keuka Lake outlet and a mile west of Seneca Lake. In 1789, the Friends sowed and harvested wheat, the first to do so in New York State—one year before wheat farmers in Canandaigua and Victor.

Unfortunately, the Friends' site and Geneva to the north were both located in the "gore," a disputed triangular area between the incorrect survey line of 1788 and the line surveyed four years later. In 1794, the Friends moved to a second location they had purchased near present-day Branchport. They named the six-square-mile plot Jerusalem, a name that remains today as the town in which the village of Branchport is located.

James Parker left the settlement about this time, when it was realized that he had poorly represented the community in his land purchases. The Publick Universal Friend and her followers named the area the Vale of Kedron, from the Bible. It is now called Guyanoga Valley.

The Universal Friend's first house in Jerusalem was a log structure to which two log additions were made. The middle building served as the meeting room for the community. Members of the settlement practiced celibacy, a practice that cost the community many members. The settlement was efficiently run. Visitors were treated hospitably.

In 1795, the Duke of Rochefoucald-Liancourt and a party of ten passed through the area on their way to Niagara Falls. The Duke observed that: "Our plates, as well as the table linen, were perfectly clean and neat. Our repast, although frugal, was better yet in quality than any, of which we had partaken, since our departure from Philadelphia; it consisted of good fresh meat, with pudding, an excellent salad, and a beverage of a peculiar yet charming flavor."[62]

The Universal Friends got along well with Native Americans. Wilkinson and her followers, Rachel Malin, David Wagener, and Enoch Malin, attended the council at Canandaigua in 1794 at which a treaty was signed with the Iroquois, ensuring peace and promoting further settlement in western New York. Wilkinson and her followers dined in Canandaigua at the home of Thomas Morris, the son of Robert Morris, the "financier of the Revolutionary War." The Universal Friend addressed the council and was given the name "Shinnewawna gis tau, ge" by the Indians. It meant "Great Woman Preacher."

Thomas Morris visited Wilkinson during the 1790s. He recorded his impressions:

> Her disciples were very orderly, sober, industrious, and some of them a well educated and intelligent set of people; and many of them possessed of handsome properties. She called herself the "Universal Friend," and would not permit herself to be designated by any other appellation. She pretended to have the revelations from heaven, in which she had been directed to devote her labors to the conversion of sinners.
>
> Her disciples placed the most unbound confidence in her, and yielded, in all things, the most implicit obedience to her mandates. She would punish those among them who were guilty of the slightest deviation from her orders. In some instances, she would order the offending culprit to wear a cowbell around his neck for weeks or months, and in no instance

was she known to be disobeyed, For some offense committed by one of her people, she banished him to Nova Scotia for three years, where he went, and from whence he returned only after the expiration of his sentence.

When any of her people killed a calf or sheep, or purchased an article of dress, the "Friend" was asked what portion of it she would have; and the answer would sometimes be, that the Lord hath need of the one-half, and sometimes the Lord hath need of the whole. Her house, her grounds, and her farms, were kept in the neatest order by her followers, who labored for her without compensation. She was attended by two young women, always neatly dressed.[63]

In 1799, five years after he had left the Friends, James Parker, who had become an Ontario County magistrate, attempted to indict Wilkinson for blasphemy. Three attempts were made to serve Parker's warrant for her arrest. On the first occasion, Wilkinson and Rachel Malin were out riding. They outrode the warrant server and stopped at a nearby house, whose owner sent the server on his way.

On the second occasion, the constable and assistant constable visited Wilkinson's home. When the men attempted to enter the house, Wilkinson and the women of her household attacked them, tore their clothing, and chased them away.

The third attempt to serve the warrant was successful. Thirty men surrounded her house at midnight to throw her in an oxcart and take her to Canandaigua. Dr. Fargo, who rode with the group, warned the men that Wilkinson's health could not withstand being carried off in a cart. However, Wilkinson agreed to appear before the next session of the Ontario County Circuit Court.

In June 1800, Wilkinson was in attendance at Canandaigua when her case was presented to a grand jury. The presiding judge ruled that blasphemy was not an indictable offense, and her case was dismissed.

In 1809, the community began the construction of a second home for Wilkinson, which wasn't finished until 1815. She lived in the home from 1814 until her death in 1819. It fell into disrepair years after her death but has been restored and is now a New York Historic Site. It is a large, three-story rectangular building in the style of a large New England farmhouse. Wilkinson's bedroom was on the southeast corner of the second floor with a beautiful view of the west branch of Keuka Lake.

Wilkinson's beliefs were difficult for outsiders to grasp. A neighbor, who was not a member of the Friends, visited her often. He attempted to draw her out to explain her beliefs, but she either quoted Scripture texts, described visions, or left him to draw his own inferences. Major Benajah Mallory, a visitor to Wilkinson's community, described his impressions:

> The followers were mostly respectable men of small property; some of them had enough to be called rich in those days. Those who had considerable property gave her part, or were at least liberal in supplying her wants. Man and wife were not separated; but they were forbidden to multiply. A few transgressed, but obtained absolution by confessing and promising not to disobey again.
>
> It was generally a well-regulated community, its members mostly lived in harmony, were temperate and industrious. They had two days of rest in the week, Saturday and Saturday. At their meetings, the Friend would generally speak, make a text speech, and exhort and give

liberty to others to speak. The Friend appeared much devoted to the interest of her followers, and was especially attentive to them in sickness.[64]

Anecdotes

Many stories were told about Wilkinson; most of them can't be substantiated. One of the earliest anecdotes was told even before Wilkinson left Rhode Island. One of the women members of Wilkinson's "family" made a fine piece of cloth patterned with small squares. When the Publick Universal Friend visited the woman at her home, she was shown the piece of cloth. Wilkinson admired the fabric. The woman, who was devoted to her leader, offered Wilkinson part of the material for her own use. The Publick Universal Friend said: "The Lord hath need of the whole piece" and walked off with it.

A frequently told story is set in many locations. One version is that after the signing of the Pickering Treaty with the Native Americans, the Universal Friend met with the Senecas at Friends' Landing on Seneca Lake, where Red Jacket, Cornplanter, the Native-American preacher Good Peter, and 500 others had encamped. Supposedly, after Good Peter preached, Wilkinson asked to have his sermon interpreted. Good Peter objected to being interpreted, saying, "If she is Christ, she knows what I said."

Another story, about her ability to walk on water, had at least eight versions involving eight bodies of water, including Keuka and Seneca Lakes. According to the story, Wilkinson called a crowd together to satisfy skeptics of her divine powers. She preached a sermon on faith and concluded with the question, "Do ye have Faith?" Then she asked, "Do you think I can do this thing (walk on water)?" The crowd responded, "We believe." "It is good," said Wilkinson, as she walked away, "If ye have faith, ye need no other evidence."

A variation of the story was also told. The crowd was gathered adjacent to the water that they came to see the

Universal Friend walk upon. In this version, they were skeptical and demanded proof that she could walk on water. While walking away, she said, "Without thy faith, I cannot do it."

Two stories bring Wilkinson's adherence to celibacy into question, both involving Judge Potter. Version one has Mrs. William Potter finding the judge in Wilkinson's private rooms and Jemima explaining that she was simply ministering to one of her lambs. Mrs. Potter is supposed to have responded: "Minister to your lambs all you want, but in the future please leave my old ram alone."

In version two, a young girl in the Universal Friend's household said that she saw Judge Potter climbing through the window of Wilkinson's bedroom in the middle of the night. She was told that it wasn't Judge Potter that she had seen but an angel. The young girl said that it may have been an angel but the angel was wearing the same kind of coat with the same kind of buttons that Judge Potter wore.

The Later Years

The last years of Wilkinson's life were difficult ones, particularly in her relationships with former members, including James Parker, who attempted to gain control of some of the settlement's increasingly valuable land. During her last years, Jemima suffered from dropsy, gained weight, and couldn't get around as easily as when she was younger and had a reputation as an excellent horsewoman.

In 1810, she had the running gear of the carriage she used in Pennsylvania taken to Canandaigua and fitted with a new body. The body was shaped like a half moon and had a star and the letters U. F. on each side, and a cross, a star, and the letters U. F. on the rear. Her carriage is now in the Carriage Museum at the Granger Homestead in Canandaigua.

Jemima Wilkinson died on July 1, 1819; the notation in the death book was: "25 minutes past 2 on the clock, the Friend went from here." Her last words were, "My friends I must soon depart—I am going—this night I leave you."[65] Her followers waited three days to see if she would rise again and then placed her in the basement on a wooden platform until they realized they were going to have to bury her. Only two of her followers knew where she was buried.

Her religious community didn't sustain itself. The fall of the community was gradual; it didn't end with her death. Rachel and Margaret Malin maintained the house on Friend Hill Road. Some of the Friend's family continued to live there, and it served as the headquarters of the community. Henry Barnes, the last of her followers, died in 1874.

Strong individualism was required to lead a group into the wilderness and to successfully establish two settlements. Historians rank Wilkinson as one of the outstanding women of the colonial period. She is sometimes compared with Mother Ann Lee of the Shakers. Although both Wilkinson and Lee endorsed celibacy, Mother Ann Lee insisted that previously married couples separate and required that the sexes be strictly segregated. Wilkinson was more lenient with her followers; she did not insist upon segregation of the sexes.

Both Lee and Wilkinson had roots in the Quaker religion. However, the followers of Mother Ann Lee tended to be of humbler origins than Wilkinson's Friends. Wilkinson placed fewer burdens on her members than Mother Ann, whose Shakers engaged in public confession and speaking in tongues as well as their agitated form of dancing.

Mother Ann Lee founded a more formal and longer lasting religious organization than Wilkinson partly because Lee had more leaders trained in theology and philosophy and were better prepared to sustain the organization than were Wilkinson's. However, Mother Ann Lee was born in England, while Wilkinson was an American. No other American-born woman religious leader approached the achievements of the Publick Universal Friend until Mary Baker Eddy founded the Church of Christ, Scientist.

Oneida Mansion House, Oneida

CHAPTER 6

John Humphrey Noyes and the Oneida Community

"For nearly thirty years the members of the Oneida Community lived secluded, dedicated, and by their own testimony, happy lives. They had unwavering faith in their own somewhat heterodox religion and in their leader, John Humphrey Noyes, whom they believed to be inspired by God. They practiced a social theory, complex marriage, which they held to be completely justified by their religious credo. They worked very hard and devoted not only their lives but all their worldly possessions to this cause. They put into actual practice the only experiment in human eugenics that has ever been tried. They lived together peacefully and lovingly. Quarreling, unkind behavior of any kind at any age was sure to bring down criticism upon the offender and hence was almost unheard of. Hurt feelings, jealousy, grudges were recognized as nothing but the offsprings of egotism. They called themselves Perfectionists or Bible Communists."[66]

Constance Noyes Robertson, *Oneida Community: The Breakup, 1876-1881*

John Humphrey Noyes—The Oneida Community

Any description of the Oneida Community must begin with a discussion of its founder, John Humphrey Noyes, a strong individual whom people were willing to follow. Mark Holloway, in the introduction to *History of American Socialisms* by John Humphrey Noyes, discusses Noyes's forceful personal characteristics:

> When the religious fire, moral courage, and good judgment of Noyes have all been given due credit, something remains unexplained— some ingredient of the personality which could exercise such thorough control over so many individuals while they were experiment- ing with one of the most explosive of psy- chophysical complexes [complex marriage]. I think that this unnamed quality can without sentimentality be called "love of life." I believe that Noyes, unlike many sectarians, was a great yea-sayer, an enhancer of life, a confident and optimistic embracer of truth and freedom, broadminded, receptive to new ideas, generous and without meanness or pettiness. There were many indications of this in Oneida Community, and there is some evidence of the same kind in the *History*.[67]

Noyes thought that unhappiness may not have been a sin, but that it was certainly a personal shortcoming. He observed that "the more we get acquainted with God, the more we shall find it our special duty to be happy."

Early Life

John Humphrey Noyes was born on September 3, 1811, in Brattleboro, Vermont, to the Honorable John Noyes and Polly Hayes Noyes, a cousin of Rutherford B. Hayes. John Noyes was a schoolteacher, a minister, and a dealer in groceries and farm commodities before being elected to the U.S. Congress. Polly Hayes was a religious woman who hoped that her first-born would enter the ministry. She had the ability to move from conceptualizing an idea to implementing the idea, a trait that she passed on to her oldest son.

Noyes was tall and slender with penetrating blue eyes, a firm jutting jaw, and a broad forehead. In his youth, he was a bit of a bully, a trait that he overcame in later years. He was an intellectual whom women found very attractive.

In 1830, Noyes graduated from Dartmouth College. He spent the following year studying law until he underwent a religious conversion after listening to Charles Grandison Finney, the foremost revivalist of his time. Noyes attended schools of theology at Andover and at Yale, where he became a Congregationalist minister in 1833. In his *Confessions of John H. Noyes*, he wrote that the fervor of the revival in New Haven "was the immediate cause of his conviction and con-version to Perfectionism."

Perfectionism and Early Followers
However, Noyes did not agree with all of the tenets of Perfectionism:

> Perfectionism, which began as an offshoot of Wesleyan Methodism, had for a number of years been preached by revivalists, especially in western New York, New England, and New Jersey, and through the Burned-over District. Although its exponents advocated the way of perfect holiness, that church which called itself perfectionist did not expect or require sinlessness of its members. To the inflexible logic of John Noyes, this made no sense.

> After months of intense study and strenuous debate not only with his fellow students but with his pastors and masters at the college [Yale], he reached his decision and made his statement: "He that committeth sin is of the devil." The next morning a fellow student came to labor with him, "Don't you commit sin?" ... John Noyes repled firmly, "No." Within a few hours the word passed through the college and the city. "Noyes says he is perfect," and on the heels of this went the report, "Noyes is crazy."[68]

From 1834 until 1844, Noyes pursued his concept of Perfectionism and advocated freedom from sin. He believed, based on his studies of the Bible, that Jesus Christ had come a second time in AD 70, at the time of the destruction of Jerusalem. Mankind had already been redeemed; therefore, Christians were absolved from the necessity of sin. Nevertheless, men and women should continually strive for perfection.

Noyes's first gathering of followers began with relatives in Putney, Vermont, and then expanded as believers came from other areas, including the George Cragin family from New York. Initially, they considered themselves revivalists and not followers of Charles Fourier, who advocated that society should be formed into self-supporting communal groups. They built a chapel and published *The Perfectionist*, one of many publications printed by Noyes and his followers over the years.

In 1838, Noyes married Harriet Holton, whose grandfather had represented Vermont in Congress. She had provided financial support to Noyes when one of his publications was in trouble. Harriet mentioned to Noyes that she was aware of a love interest who had rejected his offer of marriage and hinted to him that she would rather live with him as a sister rather than a wife. Noyes made it clear that he expected her to live with him as his wife. However, he viewed Harriet as more than a wife, as a "coworker in the Kingdom of Christ."

Founding a Community and Adopting the Concept of Complex Marriage

In 1844, Noyes and his followers adopted the concept of community living by turning over all property to the commune and by living together. Noyes envisioned a community of people living and sharing equally in the results of their labor. The formation of Noyes's community occurred fifteen years after the failure of Robert Owen's community at New Harmony, Indiana, due to the members' lack of industry and to Owen's return to his home in England.

In 1840, Ralph Waldo Emerson wrote in a letter to Thomas Carlyle in England that "we are a little wild here with numberless projects for social reform. Not a reading man but has a draft of a new community in his waistcoat pocket."[69] Between 1840 and 1850, over forty utopian communities were established in the United States.

Noyes advocated the practice of complex marriage. One difference between his community and other communities living separately from society, such as the Shakers and Jemima Wilkinson and her Friends, was that Noyes and his followers could have and raise children. Noyes's goal with the concept of complex marriage was to liberate men and women from the restrictions of monogamy and conventional marriage.

Neither monogamy nor celibacy was sanctioned by the community. Members were permitted to be intimate with anyone who was willing. Usually, the request for intimacy was conveyed by a third person. Subsequently, this became more involved with a committee giving permission. Withholding permission was used as a form of punishment.

Later, men and women who fell in love and no longer had multiple "social" partners were criticized by the community, and, if necessary, one would be sent to a satellite outpost. A form of birth control called coitus reservatus or male continence was practiced by the community. Noyes wrote that "It is the glory of man to control himself, and the Kingdom of God summons him to control all things."

The Oneida Community

In 1847, the good citizens of Putney, having heard many scandalous rumors, charged Noyes with adultery and set a date for a trial. After being released on bail, he decided that it was time to move on. He considered a property at Oneida, New York, owned by an early Perfectionist convert, Jonathan Burt. The property, which was on the Oneida Indian Preserve, had been bought from the Oneida Nation by the State of New York and was offered to settlers at reasonable prices. Burt contributed his property, and two adjacent farms were purchased by the Community. Construction of the first Mansion House, a three-story, wooden structure, thirty-five by sixty feet, was begun during the summer of 1848.

Communal care for children began at this time. Newborns were left in the care of the mother for the first year or two and were then placed in a nursery for two- to twelve-year olds, where they were cared for by housekeepers, nurses, and teachers.

In 1850, the Community faced a situation in their new location similar to what they had experienced in Putney. Complaints about the Community had been made to magistrates in both Madison and Oneida Counties. The Grand Jury in Madison County, which had jurisdiction over the Community, ignored the complaints; it considered the Community to be hardworking and operating within the law. Oneida County authorities summoned Community members to Utica to be interrogated about their activities. To end the questioning, the Community circulated a petition that virtually all of their neighbors signed:

> This is to certify that we, the undersigned, cit-
> izens of the towns of Vernon and Lenox, are
> well acquainted with the general character of
> the Oneida Community, and are willing to tes-
> tify, that we regard them as honorable busi-
> nessmen, as good neighbors, and quiet, peace-
> able citizens. We believe them to be lovers of
> justice and good order—that they are men who
> mind their own business, and in no way inter-
> fere with the rights of their neighbors. We
> regard them, so far as we know, as persons of
> good moral character; and we have no sympa-
> thy with the recent attempts to disturb their
> peace.[70]

Noyes was autocratic on the subject of religion; however, he was surprisingly egalitarian in practical questions, such as whether the Community should enter or withdraw from a particular business activity or what the size and location of a building should be. Discipline was handled either in a public meeting or a private conference by four-member Mutual Criticism committees, comprised of the community's "most spiritual and discerning judges." Women wore their hair short so that it required less of their time, and they wore short skirts and pantaloons, similar to the Amelia Bloomer costume of the women's rights movement, for ease of movement.

The Oneida Community did not have formal religious services or public prayer. Every evening, meetings were held in the Manor House parlor at which members were encouraged to discuss religious matters or other subjects of mutual interest. These evening meetings included Noyes's lectures on the social theory of Bible Communism, readings from Perfectionist publications, music practice, dancing, and lectures and discussions about the Bible.

Meeting Room, Oneida Mansion House, Oneida

The Oneida Community was described in the February 3, 1859, issue of the Community publication, *The Circular*:

> The Community consists of about 200 [it grew to 300] members, comprising men, women, youth, and children, nearly in equal proportions. They cultivate 386 acres of their own in the Towns of Lenox and Vernon, in the State of New York. The community has been established here eleven years and is self-supporting. There are two branch communities, one located at Wallingford, Connecticut, and the other at Putney, Vermont, which are also self-supporting.
>
> The Community takes its origin from religious faith and thorough devotion to the teachings of the Bible.... The social organization is that of entire Communism like that of the day of Pentecost, when "no man said that aught of the things he possessed was his own, but they held things in common." The relation of the sexes is placed, not like that of common society, on the basis of law and constraint, neither on the opposite one of mere freedom; but on that of inspiration, truly derived by communication with the spirit of God.... The object of the Community is to lead a true life.[71]

In 1861, construction of a new brick Mansion House was begun. The bricks used in its construction were made by the Community. Central steam heat was installed in the Manor House in 1869 when a new wing was added. Croquet on the lawn was popular, and the members enjoyed "family" parties and picnics. Performances by actors, choirs, and instrumental ensembles were given frequently.

Courses had been offered at Oneida since the founding of the Community; however, in 1869, an "embryo" college was established. Unfortunately, it was discontinued when it was realized how much of students' time was required away from their work tasks.

Difficult or monotonous tasks, such as typesetting, were interspersed with recreation periods, and members were encouraged to alternate mental tasks and physical labor. Large tasks, such as picking apples and berries or weeding a large garden were undertaken by "bees." All members, without regard to their ability, were entitled to an equal share of clothing, food, and shelter.

The Oneida Community became a tourist attraction. Every Fourth of July and many summer Sundays, hundreds of tourists walked around the grounds or stopped to listen to the children's choir or the Community band. They ate ice cream, drank lemonade, and consumed large dishes of everybody's favorite—strawberries and cream.

Earning Money to Sustain the Community

A key concern for the community was earning money to pay for its expenses. Initially, they raised and sold fruit, although member Henry Thacker, a knowledgeable horticulturalist, advised against it because of the microclimate. They planted cherry, peach, pear, and plum trees. While waiting for the fruit trees to mature, they tried, unsuccessfully, manufacturing gold chains. Unfortunately, Thacker was right. Their efforts in horticulture were not successful over the long term.

Later, they were successful in growing and selling vegetables such as corn, peas, and tomatoes. They sewed carpet bags and went on the road selling buttons, needles, pins, thread, and other commodities for the home. Later, members made hoes, mop handles, and palm-leaf hats. Ultimately, four businesses sustained the Community: trap manufacturing, producing silk thread, fruit-preserving, and manufacturing silverware, which didn't begin until 1877.

The Community lived frugally in its early years. Noyes took his turn working in the kitchen and milking cows. The Community's path out of financial difficulties began with an invention, an animal trap that was superior to anything available at that time, developed by member Sewall Newhouse.

Even after joining the Oneida Community, Newhouse produced and sold 200-400 traps per month. Production was very labor intensive, so Noyes offered the services of member William Inslee, an experienced machinist, to mechanize the production process. Inslee used water-powered equipment to punch out parts and to produce springs for the traps. Newhouse's one-size-fits-all design was expanded to include traps of several sizes.

By the late 1850s, 100,000 traps were being sold annually to customers such as the Hudson's Bay Company in Canada. By 1865, 275,000 traps were sold each year, requiring construction of a new production facility north of the Mansion House. Other Oneida Community inventions included the lazy Susan and mechanical devices such as a mop wringer, a potato peeler, and a washing machine for clothes.

The Community's businesses were so successful that they hired labor from outside the Community. Children were not allowed to speak to the contract laborers. The goal was to protect them from "spiritual contamination." Community children lived very protected lives with virtually no exposure to life outside the Community.

The Oneida Experiment in Human Breeding

In 1869, Noyes began an experiment in human breeding, which he called stirpiculture. Eighty members of the Oneida Community participated, including Noyes himself. He had an interest in science and had read the works of Gregor Mendel on genetics and Francis Galton, the founder of eugenics. Noyes's belief in spiritual superiority motivated him to implement what may be the only human eugenics experiment that has ever been undertaken. Parents were selected because of their spiritual development, that is, their adherence to Noyes's concepts. Noyes was the father of nine of fifty-eight children born at the Oneida Community in the experiment that lasted until 1879, when Noyes left the Community.

In 1891, Dr. Anita Newcomb McGee of John Hopkins Medical School analyzed the human breeding experiment at Oneida in the *American Anthropologist* magazine. She had interviewed and studied twenty-two stirpicults between the ages of eighteen and twenty-two living at Oneida. She observed that:

> The boys are tall—several over six feet— broad-shouldered, and finely proportioned; the girls are robust and well built.... As an index of the calibre of the offspring of stirpiculture, it may be mentioned that favorite amusement is found in a debating society of three girls and four of the boys, which meets during the summer when all are at home.... It is a surprise that in spite of their doctrinal training only a very few are church members and but one [three, according to another source] is a Perfectionist.[72]

The Beginning of the End

The Community began to break up in 1879 for a number of reasons, including:

- Noyes's physical ailments in his later years. Hearing loss and a throat condition lessened his ability to project his personality to the community.
- Noyes's choice of a successor. His son, Dr. Theodore Noyes, who had left and returned to the Community, was not a strong or charismatic leader.
- Competition from other members, particularly James Towner, who had joined the Community from a "free love" commune in New Berlin, Ohio.

- Younger members, after returning to the Community with a degree from Yale or Columbia Universities, no longer were willing to comply with Noyes's rules.
- Differences of opinion about the administration of the concept of complex marriage. Towner and his associates wanted more freedom and revised rules.
- As the Community came under pressure from outside as they had on at least two previous occasions, their stirpiculture experiment was discontinued, causing differences of opinion within the Community.

The Community reverted to the conventional concept of marriage, and women began to wear long dresses again and let their hair grow long.

In 1879, Noyes moved to Niagara Falls, Ontario, with a core group of his closest followers. Speculation was that he feared prosecution because of his complex marriage activities, particularly his "social" relationship with young women in their early teens.

He was concerned not only for himself but also for the Community. He said at the time, "I only know that indictments, imprisonment, mobs, and even deaths were in the air when I took my flight to the North." It is unlikely that Noyes would have been legally prosecuted, however.

The Community purchased a comfortable home, Stone Cottage with seven bedrooms and six acres of land, for him in Niagara Falls. He spent most of his time reading the Bible and meditating.

On January 1, 1881, the Community backed away from communism. They formed a corporation called Oneida Community, Ltd., and issued stock in the company based on the amount of money originally contributed by members and a percentage of the capital of the corporation based on the number of years that members had participated in the Community. Some members left the Community; however, the majority stayed and either worked for the new corporation or were supported by it if they were very young or very old.

In *My Father's House*, Noyes's son Pierrepont wrote:

> While the Community was writing "finis" my father gave an impressive demonstration of that genius for interpreting misfortune or disaster as victory, which heartened his followers through all the trials of their great experiment and which preserved their belief that such were merely incidents in God's inscrutable plan for educating his chosen people—preparing them for their eternal birthright.

> He [Noyes] wrote: "We made a raid into an unknown country, charted it, and returned without the loss of a single man, woman, or child." Could anything be more dramatic—a man now in his seventieth year, standing amid the ruins of his lifework, shouting "Victory."[73]

Noyes was bedridden late in 1884. On April 13, 1885, he died at Stone Cottage in Niagara Falls, Ontario, without ever returning to Oneida. His body was buried in the Community cemetery at Oneida; the burial site was marked with a simple headstone similar to those of other members of the Community. After his death, those who had moved to Ontario with him returned to Oneida to live out their years.

Oneida Ltd. Administrative Offices, Oneida

Shaker Meeting House, Watervliet

CHAPTER 7

Mother Ann Lee and the Shakers

"At Manchester, in England,
This blessed fire began,
And like a flame in stubble,
From house to house it ran:
A few at first receiv'd it,
And did their lusts forsake;
And soon their inward power
Brought on a mighty shake.

The rulers cried, 'Delusion!
Who can these Shakers be?
Are these the wild fanatics,
Bewitched by Ann Lee?
We'll stop this noise and shaking.
It never shall prevail;
We'll seize the grand deceiver,
And thrust her into jail.'"[74]

From "Mother," a hymn, *Millennial Praises*, 1813

Mother Ann Lee—The Shakers

Shakerism, one of the few religious movements in the United States led by a woman, was guided by Ann Lee, an English blacksmith's daughter and wife of a blacksmith. Jemima Wilkinson, the Publick Universal Friend, and Mary Baker Eddy, founder of the Christian Scientists, are two other women who led religious organizations in the United States. For over 200 years, Shakers in America lived simple lives in Christian communal families. In *The Shakers and the World's People*, Flo Morse describes them:

> Those who followed her to America in 1774, on the eve of the American Revolution, called her Mother Ann. "Put your hands to work and your hearts to God," she told them, inspiring the rise of nineteen industrious societies in eight states during the eighteenth and nineteenth centuries. These unique homesteads, so strange to "the world's people," as Shakers called outsiders, were heaven on earth to thousands of American converts who strove for perfection within them.

> Like angels, Mother Ann's "children" did not marry, or, like her, they gave up their marriage. They confessed their sins to their elders, and in "the kingdom come" lived as brethren and sisters, enjoying equal rights, sharing their common property, and working for the common good. At first their chastity was suspected, and their withdrawal from the outside world was feared. But in time, hard work, high principles, true charity, and honest trading earned both prosperity and respect for the United Society of Believers in Christ's Second Appearing.[75]

Shakers in England

In 1758, Ann Lee joined a society of religious dissenters in Birmingham, England, led by Quakers John and Jane Wardley, who were influenced by the Camisards, a radical sect of French Calvinists. They were called the "Shaking Quakers." One writer described the nature of their shaking: "With a mighty trembling, under which they would express the indignation of God against sin. At other times, they were affected, under the power of God, with a mighty shaking, and were occasionally exercised in singing, shouting, or walking the floor, under the influence of spiritual signs, shoving each other about—or swiftly passing and repassing each other, like clouds agitated by a mighty wind."[76]

Shaker doctrine was delineated in the Shaker Covenant in 1795, which encouraged them to improve their talents in this life and to live a "useful" life. The early Shakers lived in England in a time of change and unrest. Interest in religion was revived by the Wesleys and by evangelist George Whitefield.

On January 5, 1762, Ann Lee married Abraham Standerin [Stanley] in Manchester. Lee gave birth to four children in the early years of her marriage. The fact that none of her children survived infancy influenced her attitude about sex and marriage. Her health, both physical and mental, was adversely affected by this experience. Lee viewed the deaths of her children as a result of her "concupiscence." She avoided going to bed and slept little. She ate food that was "mean and poor" and became so weak that she had to be fed and supported by others when she walked.

In 1770, Lee had a vision that conveyed the idea to her that sexual intercourse was man's original sin. Two elements of Shaker doctrine that can be attributed to Mother Ann Lee are confession and celibacy. She was influenced by the Wardleys in including confession in Shaker doctrine, but viewing "lustful gratification of the flesh" as evil was originated by Lee.

Shakers experienced persecution and charges of fanaticism and heresy in England, and, on several occasions, members of the sect were stoned. Once Lee was struck and knocked down with clubs and then kicked by members of a mob. She was imprisoned for blasphemy and, while in prison, had a vision in which Christ appeared asking her to preach the gospel and to live a sinless life. After seeing this vision, she told her Shaker followers that: "It is not I that speak. It is Christ who dwells in me."[77] She was recognized as "John the Baptist in the female line."

Shakers in America

In May 1774, eight believers of the Shaker sect sailed for New York on the sailing ship *Mariah*. In addition to Lee, the party included her husband, Abraham; her brother, William; her niece, Nancy; and James Whittaker. The *Mariah* almost foundered during the three-month voyage when a plank loosened during a storm. The men at the pumps could not keep up with the water entering the ship through the leak.

Mother Ann told Captain Smith not to worry, "Not a hair of our heads shall perish, and we shall arrive safely in America. For I was just now sitting by the mast, and I saw a bright angel of God, through whom I received the promise."[78] Following her discussion with the captain, a large wave swept over the ship pushing the loose plank back into place, saving the vessel.

Upon their arrival in New York in August 1774, Mother Ann walked up Broadway to Queen Street (now Pearl Street) until she came to a house owned by the Cunningham family. She announced to Mrs. Cunningham, who was sitting in front of the house, "I am commissioned of the almighty God to preach the everlasting Gospel to America, and an angel commanded me to come to this house and to make a home for me and my people."[79] The Cunningham family took them in and treated them kindly. Initially, Lee was given domestic work in the house, and her husband worked in Mr. Cunningham's blacksmith shop.

However, the group encountered hard times. Abraham became ill, and Mother Ann supported them by taking in washing and ironing. When he recovered, Abraham began to frequent the taverns and, generally, to lead a life of debauchery. He asked her to renounce her vows of celibacy, which she refused to do. They went their separate ways in 1775. Mother Ann lived in abject poverty "with only a cold stove for a seat and her only morsel ... a cruse of vinegar."

Shakers Move to Niskeyuna

In 1776, believer John Hocknell purchased land at Niskeyuna (now Watervliet) near Albany. Mother Ann moved to Niskeyuna where her followers cleared the land and began to farm. Few new members were joining the Shakers, and they were becoming discouraged. Mother Ann took them into the forest for a spiritual meeting. She told them that, in her visions, she had seen "great numbers coming" and "great men coming and bowing down and confessing their sins."

In 1779 and early 1780, a strong revival moved through the area around Albany. Powerful revivals occurred among the New Light Baptists, who believed in conditional salvation and good works, in the areas around New Lebanon, New York, and Hancock, Massachusetts. One of the leaders of the revivalist movement was Joseph Meacham, a lay preacher from Enfield, Connecticut. Meacham heard of the Shakers and decided to visit the "woman of the new birth." He and two of his associates were welcomed by Mother Ann Lee, her principal disciple James Whittaker, and her followers.

Initially, Mother Ann was perceived by Meacham and his associates as calm and serious, while the dynamic Whittaker acted as spokesman. Eventually, they were impressed by Lee's strong personality and persuasive reasoning. Whittaker described the Shakers' views of sin, the importance of confession, and denial of worldly pleasures. He explained, "We have been laboring for years in the work of regeneration. We

143

have actually risen with Christ, and travel with him in the Resurrection." Meacham responded, "If you have attained to that of God, which we have not, we should be glad to share with you; for we want to find the best way to be saved."

When Whittaker explained that if they have sinned, they must confess their sins to witnesses who travel with Christ. Meacham challenged, "Are you perfect? Do you live without sin?" Whittaker explained, "The power of God, revealed in this day, does enable souls to cease from sin, and we have received that power; we have actually left off committing sin, and we live in daily obedience to the will of God." Lee counseled them: "You must forsake the marriage of the flesh or you cannot be married to the Lamb, nor have any share in the resurrection of Christ."[80]

A clear program of salvation had been presented to Meacham and his companions. As believers in Puritan traditions, they did not find it difficult to accept the concept that to purify the soul, all carnal activities must cease. After all, was not Christ himself an example for them? Adherence to Shaker tenets seemed to indicate that the millennium was in the present. Joseph Meacham was one of Mother Ann's first American converts. To him would fall the responsibility of maintaining the Shaker religion after the passing of Mother Ann.

On May 19, 1780, a solar eclipse occurred. Many people thought that the Day of Judgment had come. Northern lights appeared in the sky, and "the whole heavens appeared ... like a flaming brushheap." These incidents coupled with renewed revival activity brought many people to Niskeyuna to join the Shakers. Mother Ann's prediction of new members had come true. With the increase in their numbers, participation in labor of some sort, domestic or agricultural, was important to their survival. The Shakers strongly believed in economy and in charity.

Public meetings were held at Niskeyuna several times a day; however, practice of the Shaker religion was, to a large extent, an individual matter. The nature of their public meetings was questioned by some outsiders. Valentine Rathbun, in his *Brief Hints of a Religious Scheme*, described a meeting:

> When they meet together for their worship, they fall groaning and trembling, and everyone acts alone for himself; one will fall prostrate on the floor, another on his knees and his head in his hands; another will be muttering over articulate sounds, which neither they or anybody else understand.
>
> Some will be singing, each one his one tune; some without words, in an Indian tune, some sing jig tunes, some tunes of their own making, in an unknown mutter, which they call new tongues; some will be dancing, and others stand laughing, heartily and loudly; others will be drumming on the floor with their feet, as though a pair of drumsticks were beating a ruff on a drumhead; others will be agonizing, as though they were in great pain; others jumping up and down; others fluttering over somebody, and talking to them; others will be shooing and hissing evil spirits out of the house, 'til the different tunes, groaning, jumping, dancing, drumming, laughing, talking and fluttering, shooing and hissing, makes a perfect bedlam; this they call the worship of God.[81]

Feeding the many people flocking to Niskeyuna to join the Shakers became a serious challenge. Generally, food supply was already a problem because of the Revolutionary War. In July 1780, three Shakers were herding sheep to the Shaker colony at New Lebanon, New York, when they were stopped by some ultrapatriotic neighbors who suspected that they were supplying the British with food.

The real issue was the Shakers' refusal to bear arms in the Colonial cause. The commissioners sent the sheepherders to prison because the public had strong views about Shakers not bearing arms to defend the country and had concerns that Shakers, generally, would not abide by the laws of the State.

The commissioners, who considered the Shaker communities centers of pacificism, issued warrants for the arrest of Mother Ann and a number of her followers who were jailed in Albany. Mother Ann and her friend, Mary Partington, were moved to Poughkeepsie to be farther from the British lines. It is understandable that the commissioners would suspect that the leaders of the Shakers who had come from England would be pro-British. At least one of the imprisoned Shakers was a Tory; however, most them were released upon the payment of a bond of £100 each.

Mother Ann and Mary Partington were not released with the others. Mother Ann's brother, William Lee, appealed to General James Clinton, the military governor at Albany, for their release.

General Clinton referred the request to his brother, Governor George Clinton, who ruled that the Shakers did not intend to "alienate the minds of the people from their allegiance to the State." Mother Ann was released upon the payment of bond of £100 "for her good behavior and not saying or consenting to any matters or things inconsistent with the peace and safety of this the United States."

Mother Ann Encounters Persecution in New England
In the spring of 1781, Mother Ann and the Elders of her church traveled around New England to attract converts to her religion. Converts to Shakerism came from many communities in Massachusetts, including Bolton, Harvard, Grafton, Petersham, Shirley, and Upton. The first unrest that they encountered was in Enfield, Connecticut, at the home of David Meacham, James Meacham's brother. Accusations of

witchcraft caused the selectmen to suggest that the Shakers move on. They took the advice of the selectmen and traveled to Grafton and Stillwater.

The Shakers planned to establish communities in all New England States. Following the founding of sites in Massachusetts and Connecticut, they expanded into Maine and New Hampshire. James Jewett's property in Enfield, New Hampshire, was known as Shaker Hill; he became active in converting people to the Shaker religion. One of his converts was John Cotton of Alfred, Maine, who described the experience of his baptism after he had confessed his sins:

> The power of God came upon me, filling my soul and controlling my whole being. It raised me from my chair and under its influence I turned around, swiftly, for the space of half an hour. The door of the house was open. I was whirled through the doorway into the yard among the stones and stumps, down to the shore of the Mascoma Lake, some rods distant. On reaching the shore of the Lake that same power that led me to the water whirled me back again in like manner, and I found myself in the same chair that I had been taken from.[82]

The Shakers began to encounter persecution. During the winter of 1780-81, at the home of David Hammond in Petersham, three toughs interrupted the evening meeting and attempted to drag Mother Ann outside. Her followers held on to her tightly, and the ruffians succeeded only in tearing her dress. Later that evening, about thirty rowdies broke down the door of the house and found Mother Ann in an upstairs bedroom:

> They immediately seized her by the feet and inhumanly dragged her, feet foremost, out of

> the house and threw her into a sleigh, with as
> little ceremony as they would the dead carcass
> of a beast, and drove off, committing at the
> same time acts of inhumanity and indecency
> which even savages would be ashamed of. In
> the struggle with these inhuman wretches, she
> lost her cap and handkerchief and otherwise
> had her clothes torn in a shameful manner.
> Their pretense was to find out whether she was
> a woman or not.[83]

In August 1781, a crowd of four hundred gathered outside Square House in Harvard. Mother Ann was not there, so Elder Hocknell asked everyone to gather in a large room and to kneel down and pray for their protection:

> The mob no sooner discovered that the
> Believers were on their knees, than they
> rushed upon the doors, which were shut and
> barred, burst them open and began to seize
> upon the brethren and sisters.... Richard Treat,
> being next to the door, was the first that fell
> into their hands. They seized him by the collar,
> with such rage and fury, that they nearly sev-
> ered it from his shirt.... Thus they seized one
> after another, some by their collars, some by
> their throats, and some by the hair of their
> heads; and wherever they clinched, they kept
> hold, 'til they dragged the person out of the
> room....[84]

The mob drove about three miles out of town and made an example of James Shepard. He was whipped severely.

In New Lebanon, Shakers gathered at the farm of George Darrow, where they were attacked by citizens of the town. A mob forced the door to Darrow's farmhouse open and broke into the room in which Mother Ann was hiding. She was dragged through the doorway and thrown head first into a carriage. Father James was pulled off his horse onto a rock and fractured several ribs.

The mob took them to the local magistrate, where a mock trial was held. The Shaker leaders were released on a bond paid by the Darrow brothers and were followed by the mob until they were out of town. In September 1783, Mother Ann and her followers returned to Niskeyuna after an absence of almost two and a half years.

New Englanders of the time considered the Shakers heretics. Opinions of the populace were fed by propaganda, including *Discovery of the Wicked Machinations of the Principal Enemies of America* by Valentine and Daniel Rathbun that targeted the Shakers. People questioned Shaker doctrines of celibacy and confession, which were associated with Roman Catholicism. Also, their meetings, at which Shakers sang, shouted, shook (Shaking Quakers), and danced, alarmed the public at large.

Shaker Doctrine

The subject of community planning began to appear in Shaker literature in 1782. In a letter written by Calvin Harlow that year, the Shaker principle of joint interest is explained:

> The church at Niskeyuna before our acquaintance with them, as we were informed, held the property which they had there, as a joint interest. And after we became acquainted with them and believed their testimony, they gave us what they had gained by their industry, with the use and industry of their farm, for the good and benefit of the whole society....
>
> None were compelled, nor even desired to contribute, but such as could do it freely,

believing it to be their duty; and they were often cautioned and taught to deal justly with all men and were examined whether they were not in debt or whether their families did not stand in need of what they offered to give.

So the doctrine implies plainly, to every rational understanding, that those who went to see the Church, that were able to support ourselves, it was our duty to do it, or give as much as we received, and those who were able to do more than what was sufficient to support themselves while at the Church. For, if none were to do more than to support themselves, the poor could not have an equal privilege of the Gospel with the rich.[85]

The tenets of Shakerism in the late eighteenth century were similar to those of the "New Light" evangelical churches. Both rejected Calvin's concept of predestination, thought that the millennium was coming soon, believed that it was possible for individuals to experience the Holy Spirit, and professed that those without sin should establish communities. The Shakers not only believed in these tenets, they put them into practice. Perfectionism was inherent in Shakerism; however, their belief that individuals outside their church could not attain perfection set them apart.

Shakers shared some beliefs with the Puritans, who attempted to interpret events and naturally occurring phenomena for indications of God's direction. Shakers also tried to analyze the past in an attempt to provide guidance for the future. They shared the seeking of an "inner light" with the Quakers. Shakers recorded their spiritual experiences and included them in narratives that members wrote in the early nineteenth century.

Shaker Barn Museum, Sodus

Shakerism Without Mother Ann Lee

In July 1784, Father William Lee died at Niskeyuna. Mother Ann never recovered from her brother and closest follower's death. After years of persecution and the expenditure of considerable time and effort to protect and expand the Shaker movement, Mother Ann died on September 8, 1784. She had grown weaker in body and spirit after the death of her brother, and, although she appeared to have no disease, she gave up the fight after a lifetime of harassment and carrying heavy burdens. Just before her death, she said, "I see Brother William coming, in a golden chariot, to take me home." She was buried at Niskeyuna among her followers and had the same plain headstone that they had, except that her headstone was four inches taller.

At the time of Mother Ann's death, Shakerism had little structure and organization. Father James Whittaker delivered the eulogy for Mother Ann and assumed the mantle of leader of the Church. Elder Whittaker was a spiritual individual who was not known for his organizational ability. He did, however, work to gain converts to Shakerism. He authorized the building of the first Shaker meeting house, an unpretentious structure with a gambrel roof in New Lebanon. In July 1787, when James Whittaker died, the Church organization still lacked structure.

Joseph Meacham, one of Mother Ann's earliest converts, who had experience as a Baptist minister, became the head of the Church and provided the necessary structure for the continuation and expansion of the organization. Father Joseph organized the scattered members of the Church into families, which were formed as communities living on land owned by Shaker family members. Communal membership came into its own as Shaker doctrine during Meacham's stewardship.

He appointed Lucy Wright as First Eldress of the Shakers, thus providing the Church with a dual governing body comprised of both genders who shared equally in its leadership. Elevating women in the Church was not new with the

Shaker Cemetery, Watervliet

Shakers. The Quakers pioneered in having women preachers in England, on the Continent, and in America.

In 1796, Father Joseph died, leaving a Church that had moved from being perceived a collection of eccentrics to a structured, purposeful organization. In the following year, Mother Lucy Wright assumed the leadership of the Church and emphasized the gaining of converts and expansion beyond New England and New York State. She heard about revivals in Ohio, Indiana, Kentucky, and Tennessee and sent her followers to those states to establish Shaker communities. Shaker membership at this time was about 5,000.

Most of the communities flourished. Many observers cheered the social progress that the Shakers had made. They had no poverty and, because they had no crime, no jails. Women on the outside envied the Shaker women's sharing in the leadership of the communities. Shakers began to manufacture and sell products to obtain income to sustain themselves. They made flat brooms, brushes for the home, oval storage boxes, and furniture, such as chairs with slat backs. Among Shaker inventions were cut nails, clothespins, metal pens, a screw propeller, a rotary harrow, a threshing machine, and a turbine water wheel. They grew and distributed herbs and were the first to package and distribute garden seeds.

Declining membership was a problem. Because of their doctrine of celibacy, no children were born in the communities. The Shakers welcomed orphans and foster children; however, few stayed in the community in which they had been raised after they became young adults. Shaker membership decreased as America went through a Civil War, industrial revolution, rapid urban growth, and recessions. Seventeen Shaker communities survived into the twentieth century.

Shakerism was always known as a hands-on religion, one in which doing was more important than talking or preaching. In Mother Ann's opinion, "This Gospel will go to the end of the world, and it will not be propagated so much by preach-

Shaker Museum, Watervliet

ing as by the good works of the people."[86]

EPILOGUE

The Legacy of the Crucible of Ferment

"Just as from the strings of some aeolian harps the wind will bring forth harmonies of transcendent beauty, so others lacking resonance will give out only discords. Thus the minds and souls of men and women respond in inverse ratio to undercurrents of mental and spiritual agitation.

Such periods come and go mysteriously. The pages of history are dotted with them. They will return again as long as human beings inhabit the earth. They are marked by vital impulse toward breaking away from existing conditions. Restlessness and sense of change are prevalent—there is a straining upward after ideals that are seemingly unattainable; the public at large is unaccountably stirred and shaken—something unseen and intangible possesses it."[87]

Clara Endicott Sears, *Days of Delusion*

One of the "mystic seven," Jemima Wilkinson's Society of Universal Friends, didn't survive into the twentieth century, and another, the Brotherhood of the New Life of Thomas Harris, barely lasted into the 1900s. Mother Ann Lee's Shakers survived into the twentieth century but only one community (Sabbathday Lake, Maine) was active into the twenty-first. The Oneida Community of John Humphrey Noyes had to transform itself from a social experiment into a manufacturing enterprise to survive.

Spiritualism encountered difficult times during the last half of the nineteenth century but survived into the twenty-first century as a small, but growing religious community. William Miller's Millerites were the precursor of several Adventist movements, the largest and most successful of which is the Seventh-day Adventist Church. One of the most vibrant of the religions that were part of the "psychic highway" across New York State during the nineteenth century is Mormonism.

The Harrisites (Brotherhood of the New Life)

At the time of Harris's death in 1906, his followers numbered 2,000, including members in England and Scotland. Harris's long-term associate and biographer Arthur Cuthbert (*The Life and World-Work of Thomas Lake Harris*) attempted to keep the Brotherhood together, but Cuthbert was not the charismatic leader that Harris was.

Cuthbert died on March 25, 1914. Mrs. Jane Waring Harris struggled to sustain momentum within the Brotherhood. Upon the death of Cuthbert, she wrote:

> I am now the lone survivor of the little group gathered by Father at Wassaic in 1861.... I hear much talk of how to rope in "the man in the street" by fishing for him as well as for the learned and studious man. I cannot help feeling that this thing cannot be forced. The time

will come when hungry souls will cry out for
his Bread of Life to feed their starving hearts.
Nothing but this internal craving will create
the whirl. Any other form will only serve to
renew the storm of defamation. The Kingdom
will come as a "thief in the night."[88]

Harris had a forceful personality and was an eloquent
speaker and a talented writer—particularly of poetry.
Although his friend, Arthur Cuthbert, and his wife, Jane
Waring Harris, tried to keep the Brotherhood alive, the
Harrisite Brotherhood, in effect, died with its founder.

The Millerites
Several adventist movements grew out of the Millerite movement of the mid-nineteenth century. The largest of these is the
Seventh-day Adventist Church that evolved during the second
half of the nineteenth century.

Two months after the "Great Disappointment" of William
Miller and the Millerites on October 22, 1844, in which the
end of the world did not occur, a young woman, Ellen
Harmon, in Portland, Maine, experienced a vision from God.
Ellen was visiting a friend when she had a message from the
Lord:

> There were three other young women with
> them. Kneeling quietly at the family altar, they
> prayed together for light and guidance. As they
> prayed, Ellen Harmon felt the power of God
> come upon her as she had never felt it
> before.... Thus she entered into her first vision,
> in which were depicted the travels and trials of
> the Advent people on their way to the city of
> God.[89]

Her hope in Adventism was renewed. She looked upon
October 22, 1844, as a beginning, not as an end, and felt that

her vision marked the start of preparation for the Second Coming of Christ. A week later, Ellen had a second vision in which she was shown that she was to be God's messenger. On her travels speaking about the Adventist movement, Ellen met James White, another Adventist, with whom she had much in common. They were married on August 30, 1846. In spreading the Adventist word, Ellen and James worked with Joseph Bates, who had been a strong Millerite leader.

In the 1850s, the center of the Adventist movement was in western New York, with a large influx of members from New England. Western migration was active, and, by the late 1860s, the center of the movement had moved to the Midwest. Ellen and James lived in the East until 1855, when the headquarters of the Seventh-day Adventists was moved to Battle Creek, Michigan.

In 1860, the Adventists, who had been known as the "Sabbathkeepers," formally adopted the name Seventh-day Adventists. James White served three terms as president of the General Conference of the Seventh-day Adventist Church. Ellen and James divided their time between Michigan and the West Coast from 1872 until 1881, when James died.

Ellen worked to establish Seventh-day Adventist Churches in Europe and Australia. In 1901, she worked for the Church in the South and, two years later, helped to relocate Church headquarters to Washington, D.C. Although she was never an officer of the Church organization, she was extremely influential in the growth of the Church and was viewed as the inspiration for the movement. During her lifetime, she had over 2,000 visions. She was a strong advocate of prophecy within the Church and of making Saturday (the seventh day) the Sabbath. On July 16, 1915, Ellen White died in St. Helena, California.

The Adventist philosophy of Christianity is "to guide in the development of a balanced sense of values as revealed in the intellectual, ethical, and spiritual attitudes, to engender and nurture the desire to give selfless service to mankind" and, obviously, is characterized by the belief that Christ will return to earth as predicted in Scripture. Seventh-day Adventists base their observance of Saturday as the Sabbath on Christ's practice.

The Seventh-day Adventist Church has established general conditions for membership as follows:

- "Studying and understanding Adventist beliefs and harmonizing them into a life program.
- Keeping the seventh day as the Sabbath, from sundown Friday to sundown Saturday and refraining from unnecessary work or pleasure.
- Adherence to Bible principles of diet and health; mostly a vegetarian diet.
- Obedience to Scripture, especially the Ten Commandments.
- Strict adherence to the ultraconservative standards of the Church. Piety is expressed in abstention from drinking, gambling, dancing, movies, and all general vices. Because the human body is a spiritual holy temple on earth, the faithful should abstain from any adulterous usage that would defile the body. Sanctification of the body involves proper deportment, modesty in dress, and avoidance of unholy worldly practices.
- Baptism is required as a symbol of conversion to Christ and involves complete total immersion.
- The observance of the Lord's Supper is preceded by the rite of foot washing.
- Obligation to use talents in personal soul-winning endeavors to spread the message to all the world.
- Membership in lodges or fraternal organizations forbidden.
- Church attendance on Saturday.
- Discipline: Members are under the sacred obligation to be loyal to their affiliation and to support the program of the church."[90]

The Seventh-day Adventist Church has strong missionary and medical programs. Their first missionary was sent to Switzerland in 1874. By the middle of the twentieth century, the Church had missionaries in 185 countries. On the subject of health, Adventists are motivated by the fact the Christ spent more time healing than preaching. In 1962, the Church opened Loma Linda University in California, where there they teach medicine, nursing, and dentistry. By 1960, the Church had twenty-three hospitals and two clinics in the United States and Canada and ninety hospitals and eighty-two dispensaries and clinics in other countries around the world.

At year-end 1999, the Seventh-day Adventist Church had 10,939,182 members, 775,768 of whom joined the Church that year. One million students were enrolled in Seventh-day Adventist schools, and the total tithe figure for the year was over $1 billion.

The Church of Jesus Christ of Latter-day Saints

Mormonism flourished throughout the twentieth century. By the middle of the century, the Church had invested widely in natural resources, manufacturing, land, and owned 978 buildings, but subsequently divested itself of some of its commercial assets. The Church continues to thrive and expand in the twenty-first century. In *Mormon America: The Power and the Promise*, Richard N. Ostling and Joan K. Ostling estimated the Church's 1999 assets to be $25-30 billion with annual revenue of approximately $6 billion.

The Church considers Mormonism as not just a creed, but a way of life. Mormons are millennialists, that is, they believe in the Second Coming of Christ who will rule the world for a thousand years. Members are told not to use alcohol, tobacco, or stimulants, including caffeinated drinks.

Mormons have a unique view of baptism—that it may be performed for the living as well as the dead, by proxy. The Church maintains in Salt Lake City one of the most comprehensive genealogical libraries in existence networked to its

Mormon Temple, Palmyra

churches around the world. It contains family history information on Mormons and non-Mormons.

The Church is known for its strong missionary program. All young Mormons are expected to spend two years in missionary work. Young men volunteer for missionary assignments anywhere in the world from age twenty to twenty-two and young women from age twenty-three to twenty-five.

Frequently, they have to interrupt their education to fulfill their commitment. Their expenses are paid by their parents, over and above the ten percent annual tithe that members contribute to the Church. Adults also may be asked to become missionaries or unpaid religious administrators. They may have to disrupt a successful career, but they consider it a privilege to be asked by leaders of the Church.

In 2001, the Church of Jesus Christ of Latter-day Saints had over 11 million members, with over 60,000 missionaries around the world, who won more than 306,000 converts in 2000. The Mormon Church is one of the most successful of the religions on the "psychic highway" across New York State during the nineteenth century.

Spiritualism

The National Spiritualist Church, a registered religion founded in 1850, today has 3,500 members and is growing. Lily Dale, "the world's largest Spiritualist community," on Cassadaga Lake, near Lake Erie, began as a Spiritualist camp in 1880. It has 450 residents and receives from 22,000 to 25,000 visitors annually. Visitors are invited to renew body and spirit in tranquil surroundings through meditation or by "thought exchanges."

The stated purpose of Lily Dale Assembly as a religious corporation and as "the world's largest center for the science, philosophy, and religion of Spiritualism" is:
- To further the understanding of the science, philosophy, and religion of Spiritualism
- To promote activities and discussions concerning mod-

Angel Moroni Monument, Hill Cumorah, Palmyra

ern benevolent, charitable, literary, scientific, and civic thoughts

• To promote a greater understanding of all mankind

A nominal entrance fee entitles a visitor to a lecture in the auditorium on subjects such as past-life regression and yoga as well as a demonstration of clairvoyance. Other activities include outdoor message services, attendance at a thought exchange, and use of the library and museum. A more personalized and comprehensive message is available at a half-hour session for $30-50 in a medium's home.

Lily Dale has three dozen mediums, fifteen of whom are residents, who claim to be able to commune with the spirit world. Visitors who have a session with a medium hope to receive guidance or a message from a friend or relative who has died. A medium observed about Lily Dale that: "It is not a psychic fair. We are not here for entertainment." Tarot card readings and trances are not allowed at Lily Dale.

Another medium commented that: "More and more people who are coming to see a medium are coming for spiritual purposes.... They want to know about their spirituality; what they can do to uplift their spirituality.... This place radiates peace, love, and a gentle healing energy, and everyone feels these things."[91] The motto of the Lily Dale Assembly is: "There Is But One Power, God, the Good, Omnipotent."

The Society of Universal Friends

Jemima Wilkinson, the "Publick Universal Friend," died on July 1, 1819. In her will, she left all her land and property to her closest associates, Rachel and Margaret Malin. Her concern was for those who had served her well over the years and for Universal Friends who needed care.

The Society of Universal Friends began to decline after Wilkinson's death. Neither Rachel nor Margaret Malin was a strong leader. Another close associate, James Brown, was a capable farmer who managed the Society's business affairs well, but he was not a religious leader.

Lily Dale Museum, Lily Dale

The Malin sisters lived in the large house and maintained it for the use of the remaining "family" of Friends and as the headquarters for the Society. Rachel and Margaret held regular worship meetings there. After Wilkinson's death, many Malin relatives moved to Jerusalem. Several men moved to Jerusalem in an attempt to fill the leadership vacuum, but they did not continue Wilkinson's faith and traditions and were asked to leave.

Until she died in 1842, Margaret Malin, the stronger of the sisters, used the property as the Publick Universal Friend had intended. Margaret left her share of Wilkinson's estate to James Brown to provide for members of the household, as Wilkinson had stipulated. In 1845, after having given away many acres of land in Jerusalem to her relatives, Rachel Malin established a trust for the needy members of the Society to comply with Wilkinson's wishes. Brown managed the trust until Rachel died in 1847, when the remainder of Wilkinson's property went to Malin relatives.

James Brown, the last recognized leader of the Society of Universal Friends, died in 1863. His death marked the end of the Society, even though the last member, Henry Barnes, lived until 1874.

The Oneida Community

The Oneida Community was a social experiment that didn't survive the death of its founder. John Humphrey Noyes's associates tried to keep the Community alive, but without its powerful leader, the Community died out. Manufacturing of one of the products, silverware, with which the Oneida Community supported itself, is the legacy of the social experiment at Oneida.

Oneida Community, Ltd., the paternalistic corporation that initially was managed by old Bible Communists who were lifelong friends, was the vehicle that provided the residents of the Community with the necessary salaries and dividends for a comfortable life. The aging management did not keep up with changes in industry.

In the later years of the Bible Community, many members became caught up in Spiritualism, including John R. Lord, the president of the corporation in 1889. He used a medium to seek advice from Father John Humphrey Noyes on running the business. The advice didn't help, and the company struggled.

Fortunately for the corporation, Pierrepont Noyes, a young, savvy businessman with drive, dropped out of Colgate University and went to work at the tableware factory in Niagara Falls. Young people were not given many opportunities, so he left after a short time. He opened a wholesale business in New York City selling silverware and novelties. He soon became a salesman and jobber for Oneida Community, Ltd. In 1894, Pierrepont became a director of the corporation at the age of twenty-three. It appeared to him that the company was "sinking into a morass of elderly incompetence." He had an epiphany one day while walking through Central Park—he realized that accumulating wealth was not his goal in life.

Pierrepont rejoined the company and, after serving as superintendent of the chain and tableware factories at Niagara Falls, managed the trap factory at Oneida. In 1899, he was named general manager of Oneida Community, Ltd., at the age of twenty-nine. Except for his three-year service on the Rhineland Commission, which oversaw the Allied occupation of Germany after World War I, Pierrepont served as general manager of the corporation for twenty-seven years.

In July 1899, Pierrepont was faced with a union strike at the Niagara Falls plants. The strike and lockout lasted for ten weeks. The young general manager thought that he could provide better benefits than the union proposed. Many of the employees were in favor of joining the union like their friends at the Niagara Silver Company, a competitor. However, Pierrepont held out, and the strike was broken. He had set the tone for the company for the long term.

Oneida Ltd. Factory, Oneida

In *Oneida: Utopian Community to Modern Corporation*, Maren Lockwood Carden observes:

> In the early years of this [twentieth] century, partly by accident and partly by design, P. B. Noyes created in management alone a kind of spirit of cooperation that proved to be advantageous to both the employees and the company. The contemporary need in industry at large and at Oneida, Ltd., in particular is to repeat P. B. Noyes's achievements within the context of the whole firm by restructuring industry as John Humphrey Noyes once restructured society.[92]

Oneida's main competitor was the Meriden Britannia Corporation, which made quality, high-end silverware marketed with the Rogers name. Initially, Oneida made only less-expensive silverware because the upscale market was dominated by Rogers. However, the perceived quality of Rogers's silverware exceeded its actual quality. Oneida broke into the high-end market by using more silver in its products and by becoming recognized as having higher quality silverware than Rogers. Also, Oneida's designs were superior to Rogers's designs, and Oneida's business relationships with its jobbers and dealers were more profitable to them than their relationship with Rogers.

In January 1926, Pierrepont Noyes stepped down as general manager and was replaced by Miles E. Robertson. The corporation had grown significantly since 1894 when Pierrepont became superintendent of the Niagara Falls plants. Capital had increased from $600,000 to $6,356,000, and surplus had grown from $99,745 to $2,278,835. He had been an extremely effective general manager.

Examples of the paternalism of the Oneida Community, Ltd., were contributions for building churches in Sherrill, where they were located, as well as the payment of half the construction cost of an elementary school and a high school. Employees could buy land at reduced prices, and they received a building bonus if they built a home. The company built a baseball field, a golf course, and subsidized an athletic and social club.

In 1916, a union organizer was sent to Sherrill to unionize the corporation. He told union management that Oneida Community, Ltd., was different from any company with which they were familiar in their treatment of workers. He reported that the employees were paid well, worked a short work week, and had many benefits. He added that attempts to unionize Oneida Community, Ltd., would be unsuccessful because the workers were happy and were treated "like human beings."

In 1935, the corporation was renamed Oneida, Ltd. Outsiders began to have managerial roles within the company. By the 1960s, two-thirds of the members of the Board of Directors were from outside the corporation. In 1981, when Pierrepont Noyes, Jr., stepped down as chairman and chief executive officer, an outsider replaced him. To its comprehensive line of sterling silver and silverplate, the company added china tableware and industrial wire products. It is the largest manufacturer of stainless steel knives, forks, and spoons in the world. The company, whose stock is publicly traded, had sales of $495 million in 2000. It has come a long way from the reliance of the Oneida Community on trap manufacturing, producing silk thread, and preserving fruit to sustain itself.

The Shakers

Many changes occurred as Shakerism entered the twentieth century, including selling some of their farms, hiring outside workers, and discontinuing the manufacture of products that were no longer competitive. The sisters began to outproduce the brethren as their workshops produced women's cloaks (until 1930), baskets woven from poplar, and cloth-lined baskets. Many of their schools had to be closed. The last Shaker chair was produced in the 1940s.

Sabbathday Lake, Maine, is the last Shaker community to survive. Sister Mildred, one of last survivors at Sabbathday Lake, was saddened that the public was more interested in Shaker antiques than the religion that produced them. She exclaimed, "I don't want to be known as a piece of furniture."

SHAKER COMMUNITIES

1.	Watervliet, New York	1787-1938
2.	New Lebanon, New York	1787-1947
3.	Enfield, Connecticut	1790-1917
4.	Hancock, Massachusetts	1790-1960
5.	Harvard, Massachusetts	1791-1918
6.	Tyringham, Massachusetts	1792-1875
7.	Canterbury, New Hampshire	1792-1992
8.	Shirley, Massachusetts	1793-1908
9.	Enfield, New Hampshire	1793-1923
10.	Alfred, Maine	1793-1932
11.	Sabbathday Lake, Maine	1794-
12.	Watervliet, Ohio	1806-1910
13.	Pleasant Hill, Kentucky	1806-1910
14.	Union Village, Ohio	1806-1912
15.	South Union, Kentucky	1807-1922
16.	Gorham, Maine	1808-1819
17.	West Union, Indiana	1810-1827
18.	Savoy, Massachusetts	1817-1825
19.	North Union, Ohio	1822-1889
20.	Whitewater, Ohio	1824-1916
21.	Sodus, New York*	1826-1836
22.	Groveland, New York	1836-1895
23.	Narcoossee, Florida	1896-1911
24.	White Oak, Georgia	1898-1902

* Moved to Groveland, New York

Conclusion

In summarizing the legacy of the crucible of ferment, the words of historian Whitney R. Cross cannot be improved upon:

> Enthusiastic religion in [central and] western New York was ... heavily responsible for its own demise. Its venturesome proponents were radicals who dared to form their plan for living upon the logic of their convictions and face all consequences heroically.... The wastage, in channels leading only to self-destruction, of a potent motivation which if applied to the political, economic, and social problems of the era might have accomplished great things, is probably the chief debit in the account of religious enthusiasm.
>
> Nevertheless, the American tradition has been greatly enriched by the legacies of this kind of radicalism. The Mormon Church, several Adventist denominations, two species of Methodism, and a sprinkling of spiritualist groups survived the period.... Oneida Community was one of the most daring social experiments in our national history.
>
> Courageous nonconformity, whatever its purposes, ought of itself to constitute a precious heritage to the twentieth century [and beyond]. Finally, religious enthusiasm, even as it destroyed itself, built a path—perhaps followed by as many persons as traveled any other route—toward the more modern conceptions of liberal religion....[93]

A large number of achievers came from central and western New York in the nineteenth century despite the fact that the region was sparsely populated. Achievers from that time include:

REFORMERS / PIONEERS—Susan B. Anthony and Elizabeth Cady Stanton, founders of the women's rights movement; Antoinette Brown Blackwell, the first woman minister

PHALANTHROPISTS / INDUSTRIALISTS—George Eastman; Amory Houghton, Jr., of Corning; and John D. Rockefeller

ORGANIZERS / NOTABLES—Clara Barton, founder of the Red Cross in the U.S.; Elizabeth Blackwell, first woman physician; and Mark Twain

PRESIDENTS / STATESMEN—Grover Cleveland; Millard Fillmore; and William H. Seward, Secretary of State

LEADERS / VISIONARIES—Stephen Douglas; John Wesley Powell, western explorer; and Ezra Cornell

ENGINEERS / AGENTS OF CHANGE—Isaac Merritt Singer; Henry Robert, author of Robert's Rules of Order; and Henry Wells / William Fargo of Wells Fargo

An observation was made to a curator at an historical society museum in the region that many people of accomplishment had come from the area although the population at the time was small, the economy was agrarian, and most people lived on farms or in small villages. The curator inquired, "You know why that is, don't you, that there are so many achievers from the region?"

When asked if it were because the region had experienced revivals, social experimentation, religious fervor, and rapid economic change and also had been a hotbed of activism, the curator responded, "No, that's not the reason. It is because the earth's crust is thinner in central New York State, and the region's residents are closer to the earth's fires." When asked if that fact were documented anywhere, the curator said, with tongue in cheek, "No, it just gets passed on by word of mouth."

It is likely that the crucible of ferment that occurred in central and western New York during the nineteenth century, particularly the second and third quarters of the century, had more to do with religious, social, and economic activity in addition to various reform movements than with geology. However, the region does have geological fault lines that are susceptible to earthquakes. Who knows what the future will bring?

NOTES

Prologue

1 Ellis, David Maldwyn. *New York: State and City.* (Ithaca: Cornell UP, 1979) 156.

2 Carmer, Carl. *Listen for a Lonesome Drum: A York State Chronicle.* (New York: Farrar & Rinehart, 1936) 115.

3 Cross, Whitney R. *The Burned-over District: The Social and Intellectual History of Enthusiastic Religion in Western New York, 1800-1850.* (Ithaca: Cornell UP, 1950) 3.

4 Hudson, Winthrop S. *Religion in America: An Historical Account of the Development of American Religious Life.* (New York: Macmillan, 1981) 182-183.

5 Ellis, David Maldwyn. *New York: State and City.* (Ithaca: Cornell UP, 1979) 157-158.

6 Tyler, Alice Felt. *Freedom's Ferment: Phases of American Social History from the Colonial Period to the Outbreak of the Civil War.* (New York: Harper and Row, 1944) v.

Introduction

7 Wilson, John. *Religion in American Society: The Effective Presence.* (Englewood Cliffs: Prentice-Hall, 1978) 95.

8 Tyler, Alice Felt. *Freedom's Ferment: Phases of American Social History from the Colonial Period to the Outbreak of the Civil War.* (New York: Harper and Row, 1944) 351.

9 Cross, Whitney R. *The Burned-over District: The Social and Intellectual History of Enthusiastic Religion in Western New York, 1800-1850.* (Ithaca: Cornell UP, 1950) 117.

10 Cross, Whitney R. *The Burned-over District: The Social and Intellectual History of Enthusiastic Religion in Western New York, 1800-1850.* (Ithaca: Cornell UP, 1950) 217.

11 Ellis, David M. et al. *A Short History of New York State.* (Ithaca: Cornell UP, 1957) 308.

12 Ellis, David M. et al. *A Short History of New York State.* (Ithaca: Cornell UP, 1957) 308.

Chapter 1

13 Swainson, W. P. "Thomas Lake Harris." *Three Famous Occultists.* (Kila, Montana: Kessinger Publishing, n.d) 129, 132.

14 Schneider, Herbert W., and George Lawton. *A Prophet and a Pilgrim.*

(New York: Columbia UP, 1942) xiv-xv.

15 Schneider, Herbert W., and George Lawton. *A Prophet and a Pilgrim.* (New York: Columbia UP, 1942) 9-10.

16 Cuthbert, Arthur A. *The Life and World-Work of Thomas Lake Harris.* (Glasgow: C. W. Pearce, 1909) 115.

17 Schneider, Herbert W., and George Lawton. *A Prophet and a Pilgrim.* (New York: Columbia UP, 1942) 33.

18 Schneider, Herbert W., and George Lawton. *A Prophet and a Pilgrim.* (New York: Columbia UP, 1942) 106.

19 Schneider, Herbert W., and George Lawton. *A Prophet and a Pilgrim.* (New York: Columbia UP, 1942) 129.

20 Keyes, Willard E. Buffalo *Courier* 19 July 1891:1.

21 Schneider, Herbert W., and George Lawton. *A Prophet and a Pilgrim.* (New York: Columbia UP, 1942) 165-166.

22 Schneider, Herbert W., and George Lawton. *A Prophet and a Pilgrim.* (New York: Columbia UP, 1942) 165.

23 Schneider, Herbert W., and George Lawton. *A Prophet and a Pilgrim.* (New York: Columbia UP, 1942) 180.

24 Schneider, Herbert W., and George Lawton. *A Prophet and a Pilgrim.* (New York: Columbia UP, 1942) 264-265.

25 Schneider, Herbert W., and George Lawton. *A Prophet and a Pilgrim.* (New York: Columbia UP, 1942) 363.

Chapter 2

26 Sifakis, Carl. *American Eccentrics.* (New York: Facts on File, 1984) 63-64.

27 Rowe, David L. *Thunder and Trumpets: Millerites and Dissenting Religion In Upstate New York, 1800-1850.* (Chico, California: Scholars Press, 1985) ix.

28 Nichol, Francis D. *The Midnight Cry.* (Washington, D.C.: Review and Herald, 1944) 29-30.

29 Rowe, David L. *Thunder and Trumpets: Millerites and Dissenting Religion In Upstate New York, 1800-1850.* (Chico, California: Scholars Press, 1985) 2.

30 Nichol, Francis D. *The Midnight Cry.* (Washington, D.C.: Review and Herald, 1944) 72.

31 Nichol, Francis D. *The Midnight Cry.* (Washington, D.C.: Review and

Herald, 1944) 77.

32 Nichol, Francis D. *The Midnight Cry.* (Washington, D.C.: Review and Herald, 1944) 126.

33 Nichol, Francis D. *The Midnight Cry.* (Washington, D.C.: Review and Herald, 1944) 131.

34 Nichol, Francis D. *The Midnight Cry.* (Washington, D.C.: Review and Herald, 1944) 251.

35 Nichol, Francis D. *The Midnight Cry.* (Washington, D.C.: Review and Herald, 1944) 266.

36 Nichol, Francis D. *The Midnight Cry.* (Washington, D.C.: Review and Herald, 1944) 272.

37 Numbers, Ronald L., and Jonathan M. Butler, eds. *The Disappointed: Millerism and Millenarianism in the Nineteenth Century.* (Bloomington: Indiana UP, 1987) xv.

Chapter 3

38 Brodie, Fawn N. *No Man Knows My History: The Life of Joseph Smith, the Mormon Prophet.* (New York: Alfred A. Knopf, 1973) ix.

39 Hill, Donna. *Joseph Smith: The First Mormon.* (Garden City: Doubleday, 1977) viii.

40 *The Testimony of the Prophet Joseph Smith.* (Salt Lake City: The Church of Jesus Christ of Latter-day Saints, 1998) 2-3.

41 *The Testimony of the Prophet Joseph Smith.* (Salt Lake City: The Church of Jesus Christ of Latter-day Saints, 1998) 5-6.

42 Hill, Donna. *Joseph Smith: The First Mormon.* (Garden City: Doubleday, 1977) 76.

43 *The Book of Mormon: Another Testament of Jesus Christ.* Trans. Joseph Smith, Jun. (Salt Lake City: The Church of Jesus Christ of Latter-day Saints, 1989) Introduction, 1.

44 Brodie, Fawn N. *No Man Knows My History: The Life of Joseph Smith, the Mormon Prophet.* (New York: Alfred A. Knopf, 1973) 78-79.

45 Brodie, Fawn N. *No Man Knows My History: The Life of Joseph Smith, the Mormon Prophet.* (New York: Alfred A. Knopf, 1973) 402.

Chapter 4

46 Fornell, Earl Wesley. *The Unhappy Medium: Spiritualism and the Life of Margaret Fox.* (Austin: U of Texas P, 1964) 9.

47 Ross, Ishbel. *Charmers and Cranks: Twelve Famous American Women*

Who Defied the Conventions. (New York: Harper and Row, 1965) 89.

48 Jackson, Herbert G., Jr. *The Spirit Rappers.* (Garden City: Doubleday, 1972) 33.

49 Edmonds, I. G. *The Girls Who Talked to Ghosts: The Story of Katie and Margaretta Fox.* (New York: Holt, Rinehart and Winston, 1979) 43.

50 Jackson, Herbert G., Jr. *The Spirit Rappers.* (Garden City: Doubleday, 1972) 33.

51 Jackson, Herbert G., Jr. *The Spirit Rappers.* (Garden City: Doubleday, 1972) 85-86.

52 Jackson, Herbert G., Jr. *The Spirit Rappers.* (Garden City: Doubleday, 1972) 203-204.

53 Edmonds, I. G. *The Girls Who Talked to Ghosts: The Story of Katie and Margaretta Fox.* (New York: Holt, Rinehart and Winston, 1979) 144.

54 Carroll, Bret E. *Spiritualism in Antebellum America.* (Bloomington: Indiana UP, 1997) 3-4.

55 Nelson, Geoffrey K. *Spiritualism and Society.* (London: Routledge & Kegan Paul, 1969) 28-29.

56 Brown, Slater. *The Heyday of Spiritualism.* (New York: Hawthorn Books, 1970) 247.

Chapter 5

57 Wisbey, Herbert A., Jr. *Pioneer Prophetess: Jemima Wilkinson, the Publick Universal Friend.* (Ithaca: Cornell UP, 1964) vii.

58 Wisbey, Herbert A., Jr. *Pioneer Prophetess: Jemima Wilkinson, the Publick Universal Friend.* (Ithaca: Cornell UP, 1964) 185-186.

59 Wisbey, Herbert A., Jr. *Pioneer Prophetess: Jemima Wilkinson, the Publick Universal Friend.* (Ithaca: Cornell UP, 1964) 10.

60 Wisbey, Herbert A., Jr. *Pioneer Prophetess: Jemima Wilkinson, the Publick Universal Friend.* (Ithaca: Cornell UP, 1964) 12-13.

61 Turner, O. *History of the Pioneer Settlement of Phelps and Gorham's Purchase and Morris' Preserve.* (Rochester: William Alling, 1851) 154.

62 Wisbey, Herbert A., Jr. *Pioneer Prophetess: Jemima Wilkinson, the Publick Universal Friend.* (Ithaca: Cornell UP, 1964) 131.

63 Doty, Lockwood R. ed. *History of Livingston County.* (Jackson, Michigan, n.p., 1905) Appendix, xliii-xlv.

64 Turner, O. *History of the Pioneer Settlement of Phelps and Gorham's Purchase and Morris' Preserve.* (Rochester: William Alling, 1851) 157-158.

65 Wisbey, Herbert A., Jr. *Pioneer Prophetess: Jemima Wilkinson, the Publick Universal Friend.* (Ithaca: Cornell UP, 1964) 163.

Chapter 6

66 Robertson, Constance Noyes. *Oneida Community: The Breakup, 1876-1881.* (Syracuse: Syracuse UP, 1972) 1.

67 Noyes, John Humphrey. *History of American Socialisms.* (New York: Dover, 1966) ix.

68 Robertson, Constance Noyes. *Oneida Community: An Autobiography, 1851-1876.* (Syracuse: Syracuse UP, 1970) 5.

69 Klaw, Spencer. *Without Sin: The Life and Death of the Oneida Community.* (New York: Penquin, 1993) 51-52.

70 Robertson, Constance Noyes. *Oneida Community: An Autobiography, 1851-1876.* (Syracuse: Syracuse UP, 1970) 17.

71 Robertson, Constance Noyes. *Oneida Community: An Autobiography, 1851-1876.* (Syracuse: Syracuse UP, 1970) 16.

72 Klaw, Spencer. *Without Sin: The Life and Death of the Oneida Community.* (New York: Penquin, 1993) 210.

73 Noyes, Pierrepont B. *My Father's House: An Oneida Boyhood.* (Gloucester: Peter Smith, 1966) 176.

Chapter 7

74 Morse, Flo. *The Shakers and the World's People.* (New York: Dodd, Mead, 1980) 1.

75 Morse, Flo. *The Shakers and the World's People.* (New York: Dodd, Mead, 1980) xix.

76 Andrews, Edward Deming. *The People Called Shakers: A Search for the Perfect Society.* (New York: Dover Publications, 1963) 6.

77 Andrews, Edward Deming. *The People Called Shakers: A Search for the Perfect Society.* (New York: Dover Publications, 1963) 11

78 Andrews, Edward Deming. *The People Called Shakers: A Search for the Perfect Society.* (New York: Dover Publications, 1963) 14.

79 Andrews, Edward Deming. *The People Called Shakers: A Search for the Perfect Society.* (New York: Dover Publications, 1963) 15.

80 Andrews, Edward Deming. *The People Called Shakers: A Search for

the Perfect Society. (New York: Dover Publications, 1963) 20.

81 Andrews, Edward Deming. *The People Called Shakers: A Search for the Perfect Society.* (New York: Dover Publications, 1963) 28.

82 Andrews, Edward Deming. *The People Called Shakers: A Search for the Perfect Society.* (New York: Dover Publications, 1963) 39.

83 Andrews, Edward Deming. *The People Called Shakers: A Search for the Perfect Society.* (New York: Dover Publications, 1963) 43.

84 Andrews, Edward Deming. *The People Called Shakers: A Search for the Perfect Society.* (New York: Dover Publications, 1963) 40-41.

85 Andrews, Edward Deming. *The People Called Shakers: A Search for the Perfect Society.* (New York: Dover Publications, 1963) 48-49.

86 Morse, Flo. *The Shakers and the World's People.* (New York: Dodd, Mead, 1980) xxii.

Epilogue

87 Sears, Clara Endicott. *Days of Delusion: A Strange Bit of History.* (Boston: Houghton Mifflin, 1924) xviii.

88 Schneider, Herbert W., and George Lawton. *A Prophet and a Pilgrim.* (New York: Columbia UP, 1942) 505.

89 Jordan, Anne Devereaux. *The Seventh-day Adventists: A History.* (New York: Hippocrene Books, 1988) 47.

90 Shulman, Albert M. *The Religious Heritage of America.* (New York: A. S. Barnes, 1981) 287-288.

91 "Lily Dale: Place for Spiritual Renewal." Rochester *Democrat and Chronicle* 20 Aug 2000: 5B.

92 Carden, Maren Lockwood. *Oneida: Utopian Community to Modern Corporation.* Baltimore: Johns Hopkins Press, 1969.

93 Cross, Whitney R. *The Burned-over District: The Social and Intellectual History of Enthusiastic Religion in Western New York, 1800-1850.* (Ithaca: Cornell UP, 1950) 356.

Appendix

94 Hogue, Wilson T. *History of the Free Methodist Church of North America.* (Chicago: Free Methodist Publishing House, 1915) 320.

95 Bowen, Elias. *History of the Origin of the Free Methodist Church.* (Rochester: B. T. Roberts, 1871) 230.

96 Hogue, Wilson T. *History of the Free Methodist Church of North America.* (Chicago: Free Methodist Publishing House, 1915) 325.

APPENDIX

Other Communes and Religions along the "Psychic Highway"

Other communes and religions were founded in central and western New York during the nineteenth century, including the Amana Society, the Skaneateles Community, and the Free Methodist Church. Also, six Fourierist colonies were established in central New York in the spring of 1842. Five were in the Rochester region and a sixth was at Watertown. All of these Fourierist colonies were short-lived.

Amana Society

Members of the Amana Society emigrated from Germany with its leader, Christian Metz, in 1842. They established the Ebenezer Community on a 5,000-acre site near Buffalo. All property was held in common and owned by the commune. The Society viewed the Bible as the only authority for their social and religious behavior. The use of anything not mentioned in the Bible was prohibited, including, in later years, electricity, telephones, automobiles, farm machinery, and modern home appliances. The Ebenezer Community had no ministers; they vested authority in an elected leader. Dancing, drinking, gambling, and smoking were not allowed.

In 1854, their community was decimated by fever. They had expanded their tract of land to 9,000 acres, but no surrounding land was available for further expansion. In 1855, they moved to Iowa, near Davenport. Four years later they became known as the Amana Society. When Metz died in 1867, he was succeeded by Barbara Heineman Landmann, who was thought to have the gift of prophecy. She led them into a period of growth with a core of seven villages, fifty businesses, and a profitable farm on 25,000 acres of land.

In 1932, the Amana Society separated into economic and religious entities. The economic part became a joint stock company organized as a collective-cooperative enterprise. The religious component became the Amana Church Society.

The Amana Church Society strictly observes the Sabbath, and church attendance, consisting of prayers, readings, and testimony, is mandatory. They do not consider themselves a part of any Christian denomination. Members of the Society marry, according to Scripture, but small families are encouraged. They believe in personal confession and communion. Their beliefs include the communion of saints, remission of sins, resurrection of the body, and life everlasting. The Society has its own health care organization. Special care is provided for orphans, the disabled, and the elderly.

The Skaneateles Community

In 1843, the Skaneateles Community was formed by antislavery agent John Anderson Collins on a 300-acre farm in Mottville, north of Skaneateles. Collins, who had accompanied Frederick Douglass on lecture tours, lectured on social reform, not just slavery. Members of the Community called its site "Community Place."

Collins held preliminary meetings to review general plans for an "industrial community." The Skaneateles Community was based on the tenets of Charles Fourier, the French Socialist who advocated economic and social change by establishing small, independent farm communities in which each member owned a share of the farm. The Skaneateles Community published a biweekly newspaper, *The Communist*, with the masthead "Free Inquiry—General Progression—Common Possessions—Oneness of Interest—Universal Brotherhood."

All members worked; however, each could chose the kind of work that he or she did. Members worked four hours a day farming, gardening, printing, making shoes, or they could work in the blacksmith shop, chair factory, sawmill, or saddlery. The remainder of the day was spent gaining knowledge by drawing, reading, or studying astronomy, geography, and music.

On November 19, 1843, when Collins declared his principles, "Articles of Belief and Disbelief and Creed," in a public statement, he shocked not only the Skaneateles Community but the community at large. Article one described an atheist doctrine of disbelief in religion, church, and the Bible. Article two declared that since the organized government wasn't recognized, members didn't have to pay taxes, be subjected to jury duty, or serve in the military.

Article three stated that all members must turn over their possessions to the community treasury because all goods and property were to be held in common. Article four declared that marriage vows weren't binding, and

184

that only a public declaration, not a sanctioned marriage ceremony, united a man and woman as man and wife. Nevertheless, adultery, fornication, and promiscuity were to be avoided. Article five prohibited eating meat, drinking alcohol, and using drugs.

Many members left after the announcement of the "Articles of Belief and Disbelief and Creed." The articles against the church and marriage made them uncomfortable. In 1846, Collins abandoned the Skaneateles Community after deciding that the doctrines were ahead of their time. Many of the operating details of the Community, particularly the economic ones, couldn't be agreed upon. Collins moved to California, where he became a land auctioneer. Without its leader, the Skaneateles Community disbanded.

Free Methodist Church

At least one other religion, the Free Methodist Church, was founded in western New York in the nineteenth century in addition to the "mystic seven." In the mid-nineteenth century, Methodists were plain, unpretentious people who dressed simply, were well-behaved, and worshiped without fanfare. As membership in the church grew, however, so did the appearance of social status and wealth. Early in the second half of the century, the strict dress code became more liberal. The plainness of their form of worship also began to change, with choir, instrumental, and organ music introduced to services. Also, new churches were fancier and more expensive than the older churches. In addition, some elements of the Methodist Church appeared to tolerate slavery, and membership in secret societies was increasing. Lay conventions were convened to address these issues.

A call was sent out for a convention to meet at the home of Isaac M. Cheesebrough, in Pekin, Niagara County, on August 23, 1860, for the purpose of forming a new church. The call announced that the purpose of the convention was to adopt a discipline and to organize a Free Methodist Church on the following basis:

- "Doctrines and usages of primitive Methodism, such as
  the witness of the Spirit, entire sanctification as a state of
  grace distinct from justification, attainable instantly at
  birth; free seats, congregational singing without instru-

mental music in all cases; plainness of dress.

• An equal representation of ministers and laymen in all the councils of the Church.

• No slaveholding and no connection with secret, oath-bound societies."[94]

In *History of the Origin of the Free Methodist Church*, Elias Bowen explains the conditions that faced the sixty attendees (fifteen ministers and forty-five laymen) of the convention:

> The Free Methodist Church had its origin in necessity and not in choice. It did not grow out of a secession, nor out of an unsuccessful attempt to bring about a reform in the government of the Church. Those concerned in its formation never expected a separation from the Methodist Episcopal Church, until they were unjustly excluded from its pale. They sought redress at the proper tribunal. It was not granted. Even a candid hearing was denied them. Thus thrown out, and the possibility of a restoration being cut off, and believing that God still called them to labor for the salvation of souls, they had no alternative but to form a new organization. In doctrine, discipline, and spirit, they were Methodists, and hence they could not offer themselves to any other organization.[95]

Rev. B. T. Roberts was elected General Superintendent of the Free Methodist Church. In *History of the Free Methodist Church of North America*, Wilson T. Hogue describes how the new church was named:

> The name Methodist was assumed because they claimed to be Methodists—of the original type—in doctrine, usages, experience, and practice. They were and are John Wesley Methodists. As to the prefix Free, it signified freedom from the [Methodist] Episcopal denomination from which they had suffered in the Church which cast them out; freedom from Lodge rule

or interference, which had wrought so disastrously in the troubles which led to their expulsion; freedom from those discriminations in favor of the wealthy and aristocratic in the house of God, which are engendered by the renting or sale of pews; the freedom of the Spirit in personal experience, accompanied by freedom on the part of all, in the public worship of God, to give such outward expression to deep religious emotion as the Holy Spirit may inspire or prompt.[96]

The new church leadership spoke out against church members who "dance, play cards, attend theatres, [and] absent themselves from revivals" and, generally, against all "superficial, false, and fashionable Christians." In its early years, the Free Methodist Church was active in three areas of western New York, Illinois, and Michigan. The Church attracted members from other Protestant denominations, but most members came from the Methodist Episcopal Church.

By the 1890s, individual church memberships began to join with other church memberships to form larger groupings within the Church. Some of these groupings led the sustained growth of the Free Methodist Church into the twentieth century. In 1999, the Free Methodist Church had over 600 churches and 73,391 members in the United States, and churches in fifty-nine countries with an overseas membership of 526,977.

. . .

Mennonites
Movement of Mennonite families from Lancaster, Pennsylvania, to the Finger Lakes Region began in 1974. Movement northward was not motivated by religious or social reasons but by economic reasons. Farm land in the Finger Lakes Region sold for $500 to $1,500 an acre, compared with $5,000 to $15,000 an acre in Lancaster County. Most Mennonites moving into Yates County, as well as Schuyler, Seneca, and Ontario Counties, are members of the Groffdale Conference sect. The Penn Yan area has been a popular destination for Mennonites moving to the region. Most Mennonites have dairy farms, but they also raise hogs, beef cattle, and vegetable crops. They also make products, such as harnesses and furniture. They are pacifists, and they maintain their own school systems.

GLOSSARY

Adventism—belief in the Second Coming of Christ, that is, that God will be resurrected and physically will return to earth. With Christ's return to earth, the dead will be resurrected, and the righteous will experience eternal happiness. William Miller (1782-1849) is considered the founder of the Adventist movement in America. In 1845, shortly after Miller's "Great Disappointment" in which the world did not come to an end, Adventists formed their own organization in the United States.

Amish—followers of Jacob Ammann, the Mennonite bishop of Alsace, France, who broke with the Mennonite Church over enforcement of church discipline to form the Amish Church during the Swiss Reformation. They prohibit the use of modern technology (devices not mentioned in the Bible), and they believe in simplicity of dress and in education outside the public school system. Amish will not bear arms. They believe in the Second Coming of Christ with the accompanying establishment of the Kingdom of God.

Apocalypse—the Book of Revelation of St. John the Divine, the last book of the New Testament, or a class of writings assuming to reveal the ultimate Divine purpose that has come to be known, generally, as a prophetic disclosure or a revelation.

Apocryhpha—early Christian writings of uncertain origin not accepted by Protestants because they are not part of Hebrew Scriptures. Eleven of the fourteen biblical books included in the Vulgate as an appendix to the Old Testament have been accepted in the Roman Catholic canon.

Arminianism—based on the beliefs of James (Jacobus) Arminius who objected to the extreme dogmatism of Calvin, that is, that everything enjoyable was sinful. Arminius believed that atonement was available for all believers, not just the select few, and that one's degree of faith determined whether or not one would go to heaven.

Brook Farm—a Transcendentalist utopian community established in East Roxbury, Massachusetts, in 1841 by Unitarian minister George Ripley (1802-1880) dedicated to "a more wholesome and simple life." Ripley viewed Brook Farm as "if not the sunrise, the morning star" of a new social order in which intellectual could work alongside laborer in a non-competitive environment. Social life included concerts, picnics, and parties. However, the community was not completely self-supporting; it required outside financial help. Eventually, it became a Fourierist colony.

Calvinism—the beliefs of John Calvin (1509-1564), Protestant reformer who argued with the church establishment. His strict principles defined "Puritanism." He rejected the primacy of the Pope, purgatory, transubstantiation, absolution by priests, and all excessive indulgence. Calvin advocated the abolishment of the sacraments and the "worship" of images; he believed in celibacy. He differed with Luther over the Eucharist, which Calvin viewed as merely a symbolic rite.

Campbellites—adherents of the church founded in 1829 by Alexander Campbell. They combined with the "Christian Church" of Barton Stone in 1832 to form the "Disciples of Christ," who proposed joining with all Christians in a nondenominational organization. They were concerned about the shortcomings of sectarians and the divisions among Christians. One of their slogans was: "No creed but Christ; no book but the Bible; no name but the Divine."

Christian Scientists—followers of Mary Baker Eddy (1821-1910), who organized the First Church of Christ, Scientist, in Massachusetts in 1892. Eddy, at the age of twelve and at the age of forty-four, overcame illness and injury by prayer and Scripture reading. She studied the Bible to learn about the art of healing as practiced by Christ. She concluded that disease and illness can be overcome by man's will with spiritual help, and, if man is in harmony with the Spirit and the power of God, he does not the help of doctors, hospitals, or medicine. Members of the church believe in the Holy Trinity, the Virgin Birth, and that Christ was sent to redeem mankind from evil, hurt, and sorrow.

Church of Jesus Christ of Latter-day Saints—a church founded by Joseph Smith in Palmyra, New York, that moved to Ohio, Illinois, and Missouri before settling in Salt Lake City, Utah. Its members are called Mormons after the father of the angel Moroni, who conveyed the content of the Book of Mormon to Joseph Smith.

Clairvoyant—having a keen intuitive insight or perceptiveness, being very discerning. Possessing the ability to perceive things outside of the usual range of human senses.

Commune—a group of people living together separate from society, usually in search of a utopian society. Property is owned in common, and everyone works at the same rate of pay to support the community. The social arrangements of the Shakers and the Oneida Community were

189

examples of communes.

Cult—a religion or religious sect generally considered to be extremist. A system of religious worship with specific rites and ceremonies—a group having an exclusive ideology.

Disciples of Christ—see Campbellites

Ephrata Society—a religious commune founded in 1732 at Ephrata, Pennsylvania, by Johann Bissell (1690-1768) that split off from the Dunker movement. The Perfectionist society engaged in farming, trades, and religious activities. Initially, property was owned in common. The Ephrata Society, which, after 1814, was known as the Seventh-day Baptists, was interdenominational. They were celibate and kept the sexes separated.

Evangelists—individuals and groups who convey the message of salvation to the world. They are fundamentalists who believe in the infallibility of the Bible. They are not a denomination or an organized church but exist within most Christian denominations.

Fourierism—a social concept developed by French socialist Charles Fourier (1772-1837), in which a community was divided into phalanxes of about 1,600 people with common buildings and allotments of land for cultivation. Members were not required to turn over private property to the community, and normal family life could be maintained. Forty-one phalanxes were founded in the United States during the nineteenth century. Albert Brisbane (1809-1890) was the most important American follower of Fourier. In its later days, Brook Farm became a Fourierist community.

Fundamentalism—a Protestant movement that stresses belief in the literal truth of the Bible not only in faith and morals but also as historical record and as a source of prophecy, such as Creation and the Second Coming of Christ.

Great Awakening (First)—1725-1750—combined the Calvinism of the early American pioneers with Arminianism. Jonathan Edwards and George Whitefield preached that with faith salvation could be attained, and that true religion, which was not provided by the traditional churches, was an emotional experience.

Great Awakening (Second)—1800-1835—Arminian concepts of emotional religion spread to the expanding cities. Evangelist Charles

Grandison Finney attempted to move people back to the pious way of life of the past. He promoted simple Christian life over the evils of the industrial revolution. *1875-1914*—Dwight Moody brought the revival movement to the cities. He preached that the country had turned away from God, and that the established churches had compromised. He advocated turning away from dancing, drinking, immodest clothing, and swearing, and going back to the behavior patterns of the farm and the frontier.

Great Awakening (Third)—1910 to post-World War I—Billy Sunday preached civic reform and moral improvement in the cities. He believed in Fundamentalist Protestantism and individual self-reliance and spoke out against unionism, monopolism, and the social gospel popular at the time. He advocated a return to the simpler ways of earlier times.

Great Awakening (Fourth)—1945-1960—Billy Graham, as well as Oral Roberts and A. A. Allen, advocated a return to the fundamentals of the Christian faith to overcome personal problems and social ills. Roberts and Allen, with Pentecostal backgrounds, emphasized faith healing more than Graham. Graham's campaigns were known for their planning, organization, and adroit use of the media.

Hydropathy—the treatment of disease using water, internally and externally. Heat and cold are the active elements of the treatment; water is the media. Interest in hydropathy began in 1829 in Austria, when Vincenz Priessnitz gained fame with the results of his treatments. In addition to advocating drinking water, Priessnitz's treatments included hot and cold baths, steam baths, sitz baths, foot baths, compresses, and rubbings. Two examples of hydropathic institutes in central New York were Dr. James Jackson's "Our Home on the Hillside" that opened at Dansville 1858 and the Glen Haven Water Cure near Skaneateles that was purchased by Dr. William Thomas in 1860.

Icarians—members of a utopian commune led by the French socialist, Etienne Cabet, a disciple of Robert Owen. In 1848, Cabet and his group of socialists from France arrived in Texas. Icarian communities had no rich members; everyone had to work, and the results of their labor was shared equally. Taxes were equitable, everyone was eligible for an old-age pension, and education was emphasized. Property was owned collectively, and the communes had representative governments. In 1849, the Icarians purchased buildings and land in Nauvoo, Illinois, from the

Mormons.

Medium—a person through whom spirits of the dead are believed to communicate with the living, sometimes in séances.

Mennonites—members of a church that developed during the Protestant Reformation when it separated from the Reformed Church in Switzerland founded by Ulrich Zwingli. In 1683, several groups emigrated from Germany to Germantown, Pennsylvania. In 1710, they relocated on farms near Lancaster. They did not assimilate into communities in the area but established their own communities, where they founded their own schools. Mennonites are pacifists, and most avoid modern technology.

Mesmerism—the form of treatment of the patients of Franz Anton Mesmer (1734-1815), Austrian physician and mystic, who believed that "animal magneticism" radiating from his body was a healing power. He believed that stars influence the health and general condition of man, and that his occasional cures were due to natural phenomena. His medical colleagues believed that he practiced magic and called him a charlatan. He did not foresee the future therapeutic benefits of hypnotism and of the power of suggestion.

Millennialism—belief that transformation of the world would be triggered by the Second Coming of Christ and His establishment of the kingdom of God on earth—that God will physically return to earth accompanied by the resurrection of the dead and eternal salvation for the righteous. Premillennialists believe that Christ will return to earth, establish a new kingdom, and rule for a thousand years. Postmillennialists believe that, after a thousand years of peace, Christ will be resurrected to establish a new kingdom.

Mormonism—see Church of Jesus Christ of Latter-day Saints

Mysticism—belief in the spiritual intuition of truths thought to transcend ordinary understanding. A spiritual discipline of direct communion with Deity through meditation or contemplation. A belief in realities beyond perception and in comprehension accessible subjectively, such as by intuition.

New Harmony—see Owen, Robert

New Lights—a movement that grew out of the emotionalism of the First Great Awakening in the 1740s when Congregationialists separated into two branches. The first branch believed in the Half-way Covenant in which children of church members could become church members without experiencing conversion. The other branch, the "New Lights" led by Jonathan Edwards, believed that conversion was required for membership in the church.

Owen, Robert—British social reformer, philanthropist, millenarian, and owner of a textile mill in Scotland who had a vision involving "the construction of a great social and moral machine, calculated to produce wealth, knowledge, and happiness, with unprecedented precision and rapidity." In 1824-25, Owen founded seven communities in America. The best-known was one he bought from the German Rappite sect in New Harmony, Indiana. New Harmony adopted a constitution documenting the community ownership of property and a representative form of government. After his return to England, Owen's communities failed in the absence of his practical guidance.

Perfectionism—the concept of Christian Perfectionism, that some Christians can lead morally perfect lives, goes back to the 1100s. A French sect, the Albigensians, believed that freedom from sin could be achieved by abstaining from meat and wine, practicing celibacy, experiencing poverty, and living separately from the sinful world. John Wesley, the founder of Methodism, preached that Christians must attempt to live without sin, and that some would be successful. In the Oneida Community, John Humphrey Noyes advocated that "anyone who professed inner perfection must work to bring his outer behavior into line with his inner state by improving his moral and spiritual character, by developing his intellectual capacities, and by working to realize all his potentialities."

Phrenology—an empirical system developed about 1800 by F. J. Gall, who believed that each mental faculty is located in a specific region of the surface of the brain, and that the size of each region is critical. Phrenologists believed that they could determine the abilities and personality of people by measuring their skull. Phrenology was popular in the nineteenth century but was eventually discredited by scholarly research.

Postmillennialism—belief that Christ will return to earth AFTER the church had established the millennium by its adherence to the preachings of the Gospel, that is, that the establishment of the kingdom of God would come gradually as a product of people's Christian behavior.

Premillennialism—belief that Christ will return BEFORE the establish-

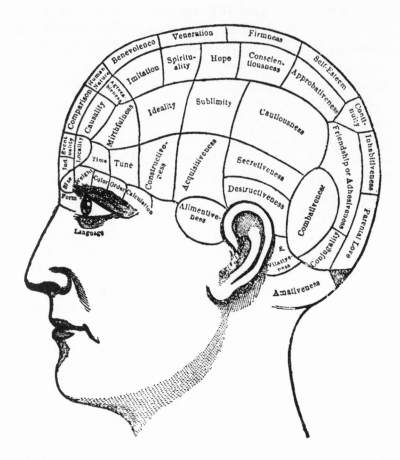

NUMBERING AND DEFINITION OF THE ORGANS.

1. AMATIVENESS, Love between the sexes.
A. CONJUGALITY, Matrimony—love of one.[etc.
2. PARENTAL LOVE Regard for offspring, pets,
3. FRIENDSHIP, Adhesiveness—sociability.
4. INHABITIVENESS, Love of home.
5. CONTINUITY, One thing at a time.
E. VITATIVENESS, Love of life.
6. COMBATIVENESS, Resistance—defence.
7. DESTRUCTIVENESS, Executiveness—force.
8. ALIMENTIVENESS, Appetite—hunger.
9. ACQUISITIVENESS, Accumulation.
10. SECRETIVENESS, Policy—management.
11. CAUTIOUSNESS Prudence—provision.
12. APPROBATIVENESS, Ambition—display.
13. SELF-ESTEEM, Self-respect—dignity.
14. FIRMNESS, Decision—perseverance.
15. CONSCIENTIOUSNESS, Justice, equity.
16. HOPE, Expectation—enterprise.
17. SPIRITUALITY, Intuition—faith—credulity.
18. VENERATION, Devotion—respect.
19. BENEVOLENCE, Kindness—goodness.

20. CONSTRUCTIVENESS, Mechanical ingenuity.
21. IDEALITY, Refinement—taste—purity.
B. SUBLIMITY, Love of grandeur—infinitude.
22. IMITATION, Copying—patterning.
23. MIRTHFULNESS, Jocoseness—wit—fun.
24. INDIVIDUALITY, Observation.
25. FORM, Recollection of shape.
26. SIZE, Measuring by the eye.
27. WEIGHT, Balancing—climbing.
28. COLOR, Judgment of colors.
29. ORDER, Method—system—arrangement.
30. CALCULATION, Mental Arithmetic.
31. LOCALITY, Recollection of places.
32. EVENTUALITY, Memory of facts.
33. TIME, Cognizance of duration.
34. TUNE, Sense of harmony and melody.
35. LANGUAGE, Expression of ideas.
36. CASUALITY, Applying causes to effect.
37. COMPARISON, Inductive reasoning
C. HUMAN NATURE, Perception of motives.
D. AGREEABLENESS—Pleasantness—suavity.

Surface Areas of the Brain by Function in Phrenology

ment of the millennium by a divine, apocryphal event. Some premillenni-alists believe that the Second Coming has already occurred and that the millennium has started, while others believe that the Second Coming is in the future.

Psychic—possessing extraordinary mental processes, such as clairvoy-ance, mental telepathy, or extrasensory perception. Involving the mind or psyche in nonphysical phenomena.

Quakerism—a movement founded by George Fox (1624-1691), a dis-senter of the Anglican Church, in England in 1652. Fox believed in a fel-lowship of the spirit in which each person had an "inner light" that per-mitted him to be his own mediator with God without any formal ritual or church organization. In 1654, two Quaker women, who could become "ministers" as well as men, were the first Quakers in the United States. In 1681, William Penn established his colony of "brotherly love" in Pennsylvania. Quakers are pacifists who have no ecclesiastical church organization. They consider themselves a "spiritual democracy." Quakers have no traditional creeds or tenets, but they believe in the Bible as the word of God.

Rappites—adherents of a theocracy that lived in communes and believed in Perfectionism. Founded by German immigrant George Rapp (1770-1847) in 1805 when he established the Harmony Society. Their celibate communes shared all personal property and assets to be free from materi-alism, which they viewed as the root of greed and selfishness. In 1824, the Rappites sold their commune at New Harmony, Indiana, to Robert Owen.

Revivalism—Charles Grandison Finney viewed revivalism as "a new beginning of obedience to God." He believed it to have five elements: conviction of sin, repentance, renewal of faith, overcoming the power of sin, and reformation of sinners. Revivalism was viewed as a confrontation with God that frequently involved a revelation. Revivalists sought a life free from sin and the expectation of a better world to come, either due to the Second Coming of Christ or to the preaching of the Gospel.

Sect—a religious body, particularly one that has split off from a larger denomination. A group establishing a unit within a larger organization due to distinctions or changes to the original beliefs or practices. A group devi-ating from the general religious tradition.

Separatists—Christians in England who left the Church of England because reform was occurring too slowly and was not thorough enough. Pilgrims that immigrated to New England were considered separatists from the Church of England.

Spiritism—a belief that involves crystal-ball gazing, fortune telling, ouija boards, and palmistry.

Spiritualism—the process of communicating with the spirits of the dead, e.g. in a séance or through a medium. A belief that emphasizes the spiritual over the material. Spiritualism is considered a religious-philosophical cult or a creedless religion. Andrew Jackson Davis (1826-1910), author of *Nature's Divine Revelations* in 1847, was the first to lecture on Spiritualism. In 1848, Kate and Margaretta Fox of Hydesville, New York, became the first mediums.

Swedenborgianism—belief in the doctrine of Swedish scientist, philosopher, and theologian Emanuel Swedenborg, who left the field of scientific research to inquire into psychical and spiritual subjects. Swedenborg wrote extensively on the interpretation of the Scripture; however, he did not found a sect. He believed that members of all church denominations could belong to his Church of the New Jerusalem (New Church) without establishing a separate organization. He considered Divine love the self-subsisting life of the universe and claimed to have witnessed the Second Coming of the Lord.

Theocracy—a form of government in which a deity regarded by priests or officials as having divine sanction is the civil ruler.

Transcendentalism—a positive idealism which held that the mind had the ability to transcend all limitations. Subscribers believed that the Divine Being was inherent in us, and they emphasized the intuitive perception of truth, i.e., that knowledge is gained from intuitive sources rather than experience. They rejected external authority. Transcendentalists in Boston and at Brook Farm in the 1840s included Bronson Alcott, William Henry Channing, Ralph Waldo Emerson, Margaret Fuller, and Henry David Thoreau.

Ultraism—also called one-idealism, was a concentration upon a specific reform cause as a cure for all ills, e.g. temperance reform could be considered a cure for brawling, corruption, marital discord, poverty, and premature death. Whitney R. Cross, author of *The Burned-over District*, did not view it as a system of belief. He described it as "a combination of activities, personalities, and attitudes creating a condition of society which could foster experimental doctrines."

Unitarianism—a movement that began as a reaction to Calvinism in England during Queen Elizabeth's reign (1558-1603). Because of their belief in the unity of the Godhead and their rejection the doctrine of the Trinity, they were persecuted by Catholics and Protestants. In 1785, the first Unitarian Church in America was established in Boston by a group that separated from the Congregationalist Church. In 1819, William Ellery Channing (1780-1842) outlined Unitarian beliefs and became known as the founder of Unitarianism. Unitarians believe that "Jesus is of one mind, one soul, and of one conscious intelligible principle, and that the mission of Jesus is that of a moral instructor to communicate goodness and holiness to cause man to depart from sin."

Universalism—an early church belief that was revived in nineteenth-century England as a reaction to Calvinism. Universalists did not believe that people could be sentenced to eternal damnation. In a universe that is beneficent and sane, they did not believe that God intended man to be consigned to eternal punishment. In 1780, John Murray (1741-1815) brought Universalism to America. Universalists shared many tenets with Unitarians. In 1961, they merged to form the Unitarian-Universalist Association.

Utopia—a place or state of socio-political perfection. Frequently associated with an ideal existing only in visions or in impractical social theory.

BIBLIOGRAPHY

Andrews, Edward Deming. *The People Called Shakers: A Search for the Perfect Society.* New York: Dover Publications, 1963.

Arrington, Leonard J. *Brigham Young: American Moses.* New York: Alfred A. Knopf, 1985.

Barkun, Michael. *Crucible of the Millennium: The Burned-Over District of New York in the 1840s.* Syracuse: Syracuse UP, 1986.

Berry, Brian J. L. *America's Utopian Experiments: Communal Havens from Long-Wave Crises.* Hanover: UP of New England, 1992.

The Book of Mormon: Another Testament of Jesus Christ. Trans. Joseph Smith, Jun. Salt Lake City: The Church of Jesus Christ of Latter-day Saints, 1989.

Bowen, Elias. *History of the Origin of the Free Methodist Church.* Rochester: B. T. Roberts, 1871.

Brandon, Ruth. *The Spiritualists: The Passion for the Occult in the Nineteenth and Twentieth Centuries.* New York: Alfred A. Knopf, 1983.

Bringhurst, Newell G. *Brigham Young and the Expanding American Frontier.* Boston: Little, Brown, 1986.

Brodie, Fawn N. *No Man Knows My History: The Life of Joseph Smith, the Mormon Prophet.* New York: Alfred A. Knopf, 1973.

Brown, Slater. *The Heyday of Spiritualism.* New York: Hawthorn Books, 1970.

Bull, Malcolm, and Keith Lockhart. *Seeking a Sanctuary: Seventh-day Adventism and the American Dream.* New York: Harper and Row, 1989.

Bushman, Claudia Lauper, and Richard Lyman Bushman. *Mormons in America.* New York: Oxford UP, 1999.

Carden, Maren Lockwood. *Oneida: Utopian Community to Modern Corporation.* Baltimore: Johns Hopkins UP, 1969.

Carmer, Carl. *Listen for a Lonesome Drum: A York State Chronicle.* New York: Farrar & Rinehart, 1936.

Carroll, Bret E. *Spiritualism in Antebellum America.* Bloomington: Indiana UP, 1997.

Cross, Whitney R. *The Burned-over District: The Social and Intellectual History of Enthusiastic Religion in Western New York, 1800-1850.* Ithaca: Cornell UP, 1950.

Cuthbert, Arthur A. *The Life and World-Work of Thomas Lake Harris.* Glasgow: C. W. Pearce, 1909.

Desroche, Henri. *The American Shakers: From Neo-Christianity to Presocialism*. Amherst: U of Massachusetts P, 1971.

Doan, Ruth Alden. *The Miller Heresy, Millennium, and American Culture*. Philadelphia: Temple UP, 1987.

Doty, Lockwood R. ed. *History of Livingston County*. Jackson, Michigan: n.p., 1905.

Edmonds, I. G. *The Girls Who Talked to Ghosts: The Story of Katie and Margaretta Fox*. New York: Holt, Rinehart and Winston, 1979.

Edmonds, Walter D. *The First Hundred Years, 1848-1948*. Oneida: Oneida Ltd., 1948.

Ellis, David Maldwyn. *New York: State and City*. Ithaca: Cornell UP, 1979.

Ellis, David M. et al. *A Short History of New York State*. Ithaca: Cornell UP, 1957.

Estlake, Allan. *The Oneida Community*. London: George Redway, 1900.

Faber, Doris. *The Perfect Life: The Shakers in America*. New York: Farrar, Straus and Giroux, 1974.

Fornell, Earl Wesley. *The Unhappy Medium: Spiritualism and the Life of Margaret Fox*. Austin: U of Texas P, 1964.

Gaustad, Edwin S., ed. *A Documentary History of Religion in America to the Civil War*. Grand Rapids: Eerdmans, 1982.

Gibbons, Francis M. *Brigham Young: Modern Moses / Prophet of God*. Salt Lake City: Deseret Book Company, 1981.

Handy, Robert T., ed. *Religion in the American Experience: The Pluralistic Style*. Columbia: U of South Carolina P, 1972.

Harris, Frank et al. *Debates on the Meaning of Life, Evolution, and Spiritualism*. Buffalo: Prometheus Books, 1993.

Harrison, J. F. C. *The Second Coming: Popular Millennialism, 1780-1850*. New Brunswick: Rutgers UP, 1979.

Herndon, Booton. *The Seventh Day: The Story of the Seventh-day Adventists*. New York: McGraw-Hill, 1960.

Hill, Donna. *Joseph Smith: The First Mormon*. Garden City: Doubleday, 1977.

Hogue, Wilson T. *History of the Free Methodist Church of North America*. Chicago: Free Methodist Publishing House, 1915.

Hudson, Winthrop S. *Religion in America: An Historical Account of the*

Development of American Religious Life. New York: Macmillan, 1981.

Jackson, Herbert G., Jr. *The Spirit Rappers*. Garden City: Doubleday, 1972.

Jacoby, Jacob E. *Two Mystic Communities in America*. Paris: Les Presses Universitaires de France, 1931.

Johnson, Paul E. *A Shopkeepers Millennium: Society and Revivals in Rochester, New York 1815-1837*. New York: Hill and Wang, 1978.

Jordan, Anne Devereaux. *The Seventh-day Adventists: A History*. New York: Hippocrene Books, 1988.

Kerr, Howard. *Mediums, Spirit-Rappers, and Roaring Radicals: Spiritualism in American Literature, 1850-1900*. Urbana: U of Illinois P, 1972.

Klaw, Spencer. *Without Sin: The Life and Death of the Oneida Community*. New York: Penquin, 1993.

Klees, Emerson. *The Erie Canal in the Finger Lakes Region*. Rochester: Friends of the Finger Lakes Publishing, 1996.

—. *People of the Finger Lakes Region*. Rochester: Friends of the Finger Lakes Publishing, 1995.

—. *Persons, Places, and Things In the Finger Lakes Region*. Rochester: Friends of the Finger Lakes Publishing, 1993, 2000.

—. *Underground Railroad Tales with Routes through the Finger Lakes Region*. Rochester: Friends of the Finger Lakes Publishing, 1997.

—. *The Women's Rights Movement and the Finger Lakes Region*. Rochester: Friends of the Finger Lakes Publishing, 1998.

Land, Gary. *Adventism in America: A History*. Grand Rapids: Eerdmans, 1986.

"Lily Dale: Place for Spiritual Renewal." Rochester *Democrat and Chronicle* 20 Aug 2000: 5B.

McHargue, Georgess. *Facts, Frauds, and Phantasms: A Survey of the Spiritualist Movement*. Garden City: Doubleday, 1972.

McLoughlin, William G., Jr. *Modern Revivalism: Charles Grandison Finney to Billy Graham*. New York: Ronald Press, 1959.

—. *Revivals, Awakenings, and Reform: An Essay on Religion and Social Change in America, 1607-1977*. Chicago: U of Chicago P, 1978.

Maxwell, C. Mervyn. *Tell It to the World: The Story of Seventh-day Adventists*. Mountain View: Pacific Press Publishing, 1977.

Moore, R. Laurance. *In Search of White Crows: Spiritualism, Parapsychology, and American Culture*. New York: Oxford UP, 1977.

Morse, Flo. *The Shakers and the World's People*. New York: Dodd, Mead, 1980.

Nelson, Geoffrey K. *Spiritualism and Society*. London: Routledge & Kegan Paul, 1969.

Nichol, Francis D. *The Midnight Cry*. Washington, D.C.: Review and Herald, 1944.

Nordhoff, Charles. *American Utopias*. Stockbridge: Berkshire House, 1993.

Noyes, John Humphrey. *Strange Cults and Utopias of 19th Century America*. New York: Dover, 1966. (Formerly titled *History of American Socialisms*)

Noyes, Pierrepont B. *A Goodly Heritage*. New York: Rinehart, 1958.

—. *My Father's House: An Oneida Boyhood*. Gloucester: Peter Smith, 1966.

Numbers, Ronald L., and Jonathan M. Butler, eds. *The Disappointed: Millerism and Millenarianism in the Nineteenth Century*. Bloomington: Indiana UP, 1987.

Palmer, Richard F., and Karl D. Butler. *Brigham Young: The New York Years*. Provo: Charles Redd Center for Western Studies at Brigham Young University, 1982.

Robertson, Constance Noyes. *Oneida Community: An Autobiography, 1851-1876*. Syracuse: Syracuse UP, 1970.

—. *Oneida Community: The Breakup, 1876-1881*. Syracuse: Syracuse UP, 1972.

Ross, Ishbel. *Charmers and Cranks: Twelve Famous American Women Who Defied the Conventions*. New York: Harper and Row, 1965.

Rowe, David L. *Thunder and Trumpets: Millerites and Dissenting Religion in Upstate New York, 1800-1850*. Chico, California: Scholars Press, 1985.

Sasson, Diane. *The Shaker Spiritual Narrative*. Knoxville: U of Tennessee P, 1983.

Schneider, Herbert W., and George Lawton. *A Prophet and a Pilgrim*. New York: Columbia UP, 1942.

Sears, Clara Endicott. *Days of Delusion: A Strange Bit of History*. Boston:

Houghton Mifflin, 1924.

Shipps, Jan. *Mormonism: The Story of a New Religious Tradition.* Urbana: U of Illinois P, 1985.

Shulman, Albert M. *The Religious Heritage of America.* New York: A. S. Barnes, 1981.

Sifakis, Carl. *American Eccentrics.* New York: Facts on File, 1984.

Spence, Hartzell. *The Story of America's Religions.* New York: Holt, Rinehart and Winston, 1960.

Stein, Stephen J. *The Shaker Experience in America: A History of the United Society of Believers.* New Haven: Yale UP, 1992.

Swainson, W. P. *"Thomas Lake Harris." Three Famous Occultists.* Kila, Montana: Kessinger Publishing, n.d.

Taves, Ernest H. *This Is the Place: Brigham Young and the New Zion.* Buffalo: Prometheus Books, 1991.

The Testimony of the Prophet Joseph Smith. Salt Lake City: The Church of Jesus Christ of Latter-day Saints, 1998.

Turner, O. *History of the Pioneer Settlement of Phelps and Gorham's Purchase and Morris' Preserve.* Rochester: William Alling, 1851.

Tyler, Alice Felt. *Freedom's Ferment: Phases of American Social History from the Colonial Period to the Outbreak of the Civil War.* New York: Harper and Row, 1944.

Underhill, A. Leah. *The Missing Link in Modern Spiritualism.* New York: Thomas R. Knox, 1885.

Webber, Timothy P. *Living in the Shadow of the Second Coming: American Premillennialism, 1875-1982.* Chicago: U of Chicago P, 1987.

Weisberger, Bernard A. *They Gathered at the River: The Story of the Great Revivalists and Their Impact Upon Religion in America.* Boston: Little, Brown, 1958.

Wilson, Bryan. *Magic and the Millennium.* New York: Harper and Row, 1973.

Wilson, John. *Religion in American Society: The Effective Presence.* Englewood Cliffs: Prentice-Hall, 1978.

Wisbey, Herbert A., Jr. *Pioneer Prophetess: Jemima Wilkinson, the Publick Universal Friend.* Ithaca: Cornell UP, 1964.

INDEX